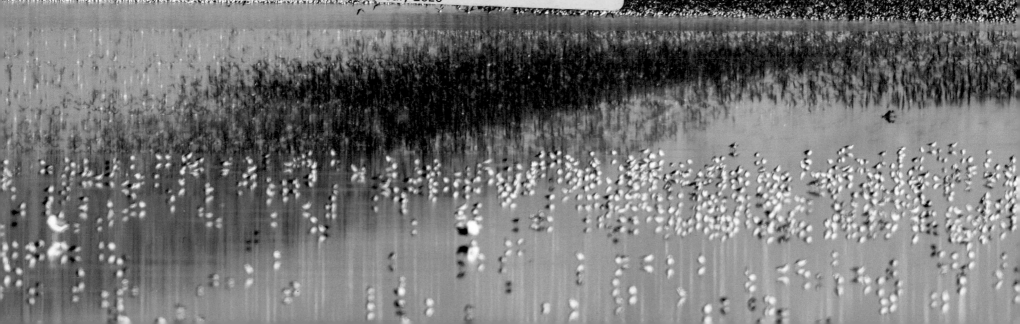

Pacific Flyway

Printed in China

SASQUATCH BOOKS with colophon is a registered trademark of Penguin Random House LLC

24 23 22 21 20   9 8 7 6 5 4 3 2 1

Cloud Ridge Publishing
Publisher: Audrey DeLella Benedict
Project manager and photo editor: Wendy Shattil
Design: Ann W. Douden
Editor: Alice Levine

Library of Congress Cataloging-in-Publication Data is available.

ISBN: 978-1-63217-134-4

Sasquatch Books
1904 Third Avenue, Suite 710
Seattle, WA 98101

SasquatchBooks.com

Pacific Flyway

Waterbird Migration from the Arctic to Tierra del Fuego

AUDREY DELELLA BENEDICT | GEOFFREY A. HAMMERSON | ROBERT W. BUTLER

To the researchers, photographers, writers, and conservationists who have dedicated their lives to illuminating the wonders of the natural world. —ADB

For Orion and Novaluna, the next generation. May your skies be filled with feathered marvels. —GH

Dedicated to all the scientists who revealed how birds migrate, and to all who are inspired by our words to wonder why. —RB

CONTENTS

Water Spirits

Imagine a vast and powerful Arctic landscape—Beringia—stretching to infinity in all directions. You are standing at the threshold of the Bering Sea, intimately connected to a world where survival requires adaptations to a harsh climate and an equally hostile land and sea. At least 25,000 years ago, when the Ancient Beringians are thought to have embarked on their journey from northeastern Asia to North America, the seasonal behaviors of Arctic-breeding waterbirds were already woven into the fabric of life.

The Beringians, who shared their tundra world with a hunter's bounty of waterbirds and an Ice Age bestiary that included woolly mammoths, musk ox, and caribou, were also skilled mariners, capable of covering enormous distances in their seaworthy skin boats. Could the southbound migrations of the geese, cranes, and ducks that they depended on for food have inspired some to launch their boats and follow in the wake of these birds—embarking on epic journeys that would eventually explore the western edges of the New World from the Arctic to Tierra del Fuego? We can imagine one such story . . .

In early spring, just as the winter's snow begins to melt, successive waves of snow geese can be seen flying across the still-brown Arctic tundra to reach their nesting grounds in northwestern Alaska.

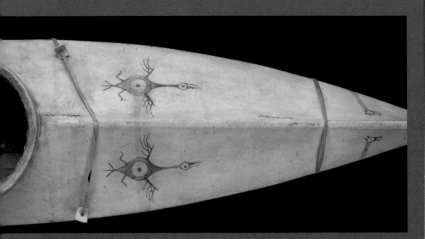

The skin kayak was a primary means of transportation all along the Bering Sea coast, allowing Yup'ik hunters access to a diverse array of food resources. Kayaks were not viewed as inanimate possessions, and the kayak frame was referred to as bones (enret) and its covering as skin (amiq). Each kayak was built to match the body measurements of its owner and decorated with his father's designs, such as the bird design on this kayak's hull. The kayak and hunter were joined in death as in life. (Courtesy of the Burke Museum, University of Washington).

In the half-light that signals winter's end in the Arctic, the white rim of the visible world appears and disappears as if in a dream. Although the winter tundra seems frozen in time, the quickening pulse of life that announces spring—a time of rebirth and emergence—arrives with a tsunami of migratory waterbirds.

Anticipating spring, the Yup'ik elders tell the children stories of the flying water spirits—the seabirds, geese, swans, loons, and ducks—that will return from the place where they go when the snow comes and the sea freezes over. They explain that all waterbird spirits, but especially those that fly underwater, live in three worlds—the air, the water, and the land.

Watching as the spring sun rises higher above the horizon, the hunters imagine the great winds that must be guiding the water spirits to their Arctic home. They know that the winter's supply of dried fish and seal meat, of berries and seaweed, is nearly gone. Spring has always been a time when the people must share what little food remains and wait patiently for the arrival of the snow geese, who will bring gifts of food. The men have been preparing their kayaks for when the sea ice breaks up and they can go out to hunt seals and begin fishing again.

In the Yup'ik worldview water spirits are considered companion guides and partners in survival. Hunters strive for oneness with all animals when they are on the water. Underneath their waterproof anoraks, made of seal or walrus intestines, they wear warm parkas made of goose and seabird skins. Paddling among the ice floes, the hunters wear bentwood hats painted with white clay and decorated with the image of a seabird's head. The hats protect their eyes from salt spray, but more importantly they hide their faces, camouflaging the hunters as they watch for seals to appear.

This classic Yup'ik bentwood hat was made in 1879 and used by hunters traveling by kayak. It is thought that the bird head designs were meant to mimic seabirds perched on ice floes, enabling the hunters to get closer to their prey. (Courtesy of the Smithsonian Museum)

This Yup'ik murre-skin parka is made from thirty-five whole common murre skins and seven split skins. Thick bird-skin parkas like this were ideal winter wear but were also used during cold weather in spring summer and fall. (Courtesy of the Burke Museum, University of Washington)

Morning fog vanishes and the tundra opens its arms to cloudless cerulean skies. The sun's warmth will soon melt the lingering snow and reveal the first green shoots of the cotton grass that snow geese love. The geese are tuned to the earth's ancient rhythms, riding the emerging wave of succulent green growth north to their nesting grounds. On the offshore islands the hunters can see dark roiling clouds of seabirds—murres, auklets, puffins, and cormorants—claiming their cliff-edge nesting spots.

The Yup'ik hear the snow geese long before they see them—a vibrant cacophony of *ka-ngok, ka-ngok,* *ka-ngok* calls echoing across the waters. The first armada of silhouettes appears on the horizon, followed by another and another. Transfixed, the people watch as the great white flock passes overhead and begins swirling down from the sky like a winter blizzard. It is a time to rejoice, but it is also wise to be patient and let the geese find their mates and rightful places on the tundra undisturbed. Perhaps this will be the year, when the geese become restless at the end of summer, that the people will pack their umiaks and kayaks and follow the water spirits to their winter home.

Pairs of snow geese aggressively defend their nests, but Arctic foxes still manage to extract their share. The foxes cache most of the eggs in shallow holes in the cold tundra soil. When the fox pups begin to explore, they will benefit from the buried treasure of refrigerated goose eggs.

Epic Journeys

Watching the springtime waves of migratory waterbirds heading north to their nesting grounds celebrates one of nature's most compelling dramas. Along the length and breadth of the western Americas, this torrent of vernal energy builds in intensity as successive flocks of migrants spread across the horizon like a braided river, some birds eddying out to rest and replenish, others pushing on relentlessly to begin their breeding season. With their biannual continent-spanning migrations—epic journeys by any measure—these feathered ambassadors exemplify the extraordinary connectedness, complexity, and wonder of the natural world.

With Mount Shasta lit by dawn's alpenglow, snow geese lift off an ice-rimmed wetland in the Lower Klamath National Wildlife Refuge (California-Oregon border).

A shorebird researcher at work at
Bahía Lomas, Chile.

Migrating birds tug at our imaginations with a compelling urgency. Why do some birds migrate while others do not? Where do they go? How do they find their way? To answer these questions, we share the amazing stories of migratory waterbirds—gathered from a cast of characters that includes shorebirds, seabirds, gulls, terns, ducks, geese, and swans. Waterbirds impress us with their ability to convert food, air, and water into a mileage plan that has few equals in the animal world. With their mastery of flight and their ability to adapt to a stunning diversity of ecological niches, these globe-trotters have traveled billions of miles over the millennia—all while making it look deceptively easy.

Migration is one of the most remarkable evolutionary outcomes in the history of life on earth. Fossil evidence suggests that bird migration was a widespread phenomenon by the late Eocene Epoch, about 40 million years ago. With supreme mastery of flight, birds have colonized every continent and exploited nearly every environment. Over this vast span of time, the seasonal rhythm of life for migratory birds has been shaped and reshaped countless times by a suite of anatomical, physiological, and behavioral characteristics that evolved in response to the earth's many cycles of environmental change.

Since humans first noted the seasonal appearance and disappearance of birds, the mystique of bird migration has been a source of wonder and inspiration. A quote from Albert Einstein comes to mind: "The most beautiful thing we can experience is the mysterious." There will always be an element of the mysterious when we think about what it would be like to travel these sky pathways with the millions of waterbirds whose lives are lived so large that they must crisscross continents and oceans in order to survive—risking all for the chance to reproduce. In the harsh calculus of evolution, it is the only currency that matters for them.

The lives of all birds, whether migratory or not, revolve around adaptations that help ensure survival, the ability to cope with environmental challenges, and successful reproduction. Of the roughly 10,000 species of birds in the world, about 4,000 are migratory. In North America more than half of the over 700 species of breeding birds are migratory. Migration flights can have a high energetic cost, but they allow birds to reach distant places where they have the best chance of surviving and successfully raising their offspring. Most nonmigratory birds live year-round in tropical or temperate environments, where opportunities for shelter abound and food resources are relatively predictable, requiring minimal foraging distances.

The distances migratory birds travel between their breeding and nonbreeding grounds vary widely and are unique to each species. In the Northern Hemisphere most migratory birds breed in northerly latitudes where they can take advantage of longer hours of daylight, burgeoning insect populations, emerging green shoots and buds, and the abundance of habitats available for nesting. Although most species respond to the onset of winter conditions and dwindling food resources by migrating to more southerly latitudes in late summer and early autumn, some species are well adapted to withstand freezing temperatures as long as shelter and adequate food are available.

Snow geese settle down on a foggy morning at a marsh in California's Merced National Wildlife Refuge.

Black-legged kittiwakes feasting on sand lance and capelin

In the long arc of their journeys, migratory waterbirds have become important sentinels of ecosystem health in our changing world. All migratory birds face a daunting array of survival challenges compounded by widespread habitat loss and degradation resulting from global climate change and unparalleled levels of human disturbance. Waterbirds are especially vulnerable because of the relentless pace of human exploitation of shores and wetlands and the associated pollution. Despite all these threats, harrowing dramas continue to play out twice a year as millions of migratory birds navigate vast distances in an unwavering quest to survive and breed. Our book is a celebration of the magnificence, complexity, and mystery of waterbird migration, but it is also an urgent call for conservation action and stewardship.

CHAPTER 1

A Waterbird's View

I came to think of migrations as breath, as the land breathing.
In spring a great inhalation of light and animals.
The long-bated breath of summer. And an exhalation
that propelled them all south in the fall.

—Barry Lopez, *Arctic Dreams*

Yukon Delta National Wildlife Refuge

Rivers of migrating waterbirds spread across the sky, rising and falling along the distant horizon with a fluid symmetry that they alone have mastered. Where will they stop to rest and refuel as their journey unfolds? We want to travel with them, to experience the magnificence of this borderless migratory corridor from the air and see the world as they do—a global geography from the Arctic to the fringes of the Antarctic, encompassing some of the greatest climatic and topographic extremes on the earth.

A trio of trumpeter swans nears the northern end of their migration route in Alaska.

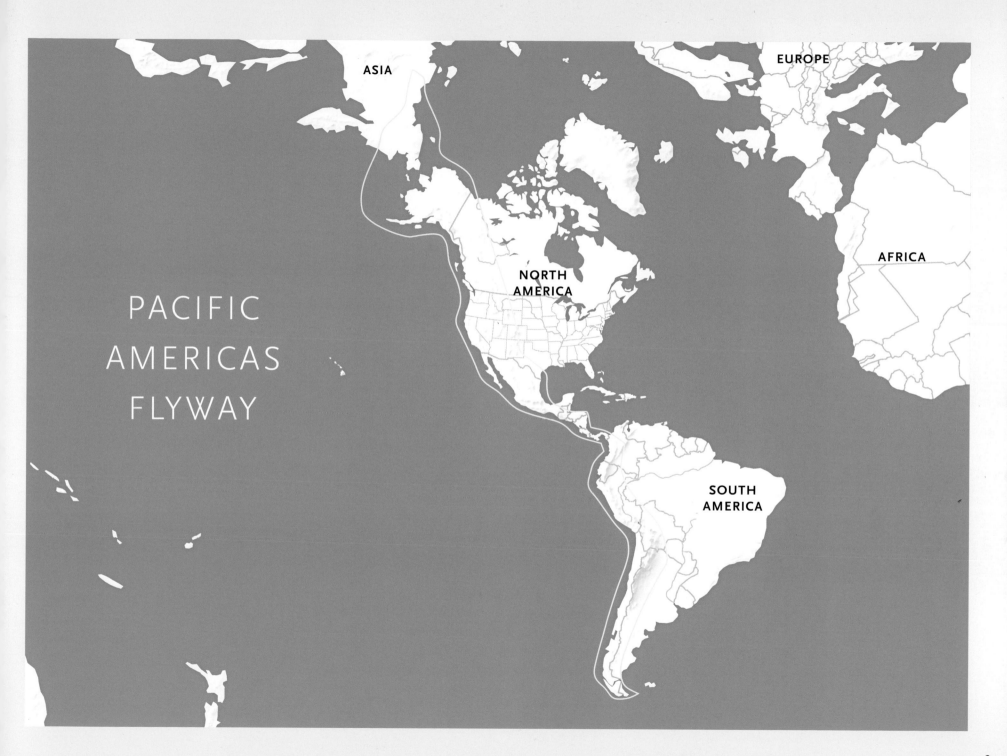

PACIFIC
AMERICAS
FLYWAY

ASIA

EUROPE

AFRICA

NORTH
AMERICA

SOUTH
AMERICA

The essential geography of the Pacific Flyway is defined by water—a sweeping expanse of coastal and offshore marine waters and an archipelago of freshwater wetland ecosystems. The Pacific Flyway, known internationally as the Pacific Americas Flyway, offers waterbirds a magnificent array of marine and terrestrial ecosystems that extends from the Arctic and subarctic regions of northeastern Russia, Alaska, and western Canada and extends south along the Pacific seaboard to the southernmost tip of South America and the northern fringes of Antarctica. The flyway itself is a borderless mélange of migration routes and intersecting flight plans, many of which extend far beyond the confines of the Pacific Americas. Hemispheric in scope, this integrated network of ecosystems is linked by its moving parts—the millions of migratory birds whose lives depend on this 10,000-mile (16,000-km) corridor.

SKY PATHWAYS

For many people, the word "flyway" conjures up the image of a well-defined aerial highway that migratory birds travel in moving between their breeding and overwintering areas. The reality is far more complex, and the challenge for biologists is to understand the conservation implications of the far-flung travels of migratory birds. The pioneering research responsible for the creation of the North American flyway system began in the 1930s, in response to decades of unregulated hunting and waterfowl population declines nationwide. The researchers noted a strong correlation between waterfowl migration routes and the basically north–south orientation of North America's coastlines, major mountain ranges, and the inland network of wetlands and waterways. Based solely on the migratory movements of waterfowl, four major flyways were identified for North America—the Pacific, Central, Mississippi, and Atlantic.

A flock of western sandpipers takes off from the
Stikine River, Alaska, during spring migration.

5

The most important outcome of this research, which goes far beyond simply identifying routes on a map, was the realization that birds depended on wetlands and other habitats used throughout the year and along their *entire* migratory route. Pristine conditions on the breeding grounds means little if critical habitat elsewhere is degraded or destroyed. This holistic view became the focus for range-wide conservation action.

The North American flyway system provided the conceptual basis for identifying a global network of flyways that delineates the movements not only of waterfowl but of all migratory bird species. The global flyway system provides a framework for understanding and roughly organizing the dazzling patterns and complexity of bird migration. By encompassing nesting grounds, migration refueling stops, and wintering areas, our evolving understanding of the interconnectedness of the global landscape in the life histories of migratory waterbirds underscores the importance of conservation efforts that focus on the entire spectrum of a migrant's journey—across seasons and from a hemispheric perspective.

The migratory journeys of waterbirds along the Pacific Flyway are as varied as the species that undertake them—an ever-changing behavioral and ecological tapestry woven over millennia. The routes, distances traveled, and behavioral strategies are not only unique to each species, but differences also often exist among adults and juveniles of the same species. Fidelity to any specific route or even to a single global flyway system is relatively uncommon and differences may exist even among individuals of the same species. Ultimately, migration pathways reflect an ecological balance sheet that maximizes survival and breeding success across the varied opportunities and daunting challenges of the flyway landscape.

Many migratory waterbirds traverse the vast fetch of the Pacific Ocean or fly with apparent ease across towering mountain ranges and blistering-hot deserts, often diverging from the generalized migration and distribution patterns we see delineated on flyway maps. Several waterbird populations that breed in the Arctic regions of western North America completely abandon the flyway in winter and follow astonishing migratory pathways that may end up on the shores of the Atlantic Ocean. Others that nest in the northern latitudes of the Atlantic Flyway may use portions of the Pacific Flyway during the nonbreeding season.

Black-necked stilts

1 Wrangel Island (Russia)

3 National Petroleum Reserve (Alaska)

8 Yukon Delta National Wildlife Refuge (Alaska)

7 Pribilof Islands (Alaska)

2 Izembek Lagoon (Alaska)

9 Kachemak Bay (Alaska)

10 Copper River Delta (Alaska)

11 Stikine River Delta (Alaska)

12 Fraser River Estuary (British Columbia)

13 Grays Harbor Estuary (Washington)

14 Willapa Bay and Long Beach Peninsula (Washington)

15 Klamath Basin (Oregon, California)

23 Great Salt Lake (Utah)

16 Humboldt Bay National Wildlife Refuge (California)

17 Sacramento Valley (California)

18 San Francisco Bay (California)

19 The Grasslands (California)

20 Lahontan Valley Wetlands (Nevada)

21 Mono Lake (California)

22 Owens Lake (California)

24 Alto Golfo de California y Delta del Río Colorado (Sonora, Baja California)

25 Golfo de Santa Clara (Sonora)

26 Complejo Lagunar Ojo de Liebre (Baja California Sur)

27 Complejo San Ignacio (Baja California Sur)

28 Bahía de Tóbari (Sonora)

29 Bahía de Santa María (Sinaloa)

30 Ensenada de Pabellones (Sinaloa)

31 Marismas Nacionales (Nayarit)

4 Arctic National Wildlife Refuge (Alaska)

5 Mackenzie River Delta (Northwest Territories)

6 Banks Island (Northwest Territories)

NORTH AMERICA

HAWAII

CENTRAL AMERICA

32 Delta del Estero Real (Nicaragua)

33 Parte Alta de la Bahía de Panama (Panama)

34 Delta del Río Iscuandé (Colombia)

35 Lagunas de Ecuasal (Ecuador)

36 Manglares de San Pedro de Vice (Peru)

37 Estuario de Virrilá (Peru)

38 Reserva Nacional de Paracas (Peru)

39 Humedal del Río Lluta (Chile)

40 Monumento Natural Laguna de los Pozuelos (Argentina)

41 Laguna Mar Chiquita (Argentina)

42 Desembocadura y Estuario del Río Maipo (Chile)

43 Humedales de Maullín (Chile)

44 Humedales Orientales de Chiloé (Chile)

45 Estuario del Río Gallegos (Argentina)

46 Bahía Lomas (Chile)

47 Costa Atlántica de Tierra del Fuego (Argentina)

SOUTH AMERICA

MIGRATION HOT SPOTS ALONG THE PACIFIC FLYWAY

The vibrant dance between ocean, air, and land creates some of the most biologically productive ecosystems on the earth—a series of breeding and "migration hot spots" that attract migratory waterbirds from both the Northern and Southern Hemispheres. The broad geographic span of the Pacific Flyway encompasses a bird-linked assemblage of crucial habitats and ecosystems. The tundra, taiga, wetlands, and shores of the far northern latitudes provide places to breed for an astounding number of waterbirds. Farther south, ocean-edge mudflats, beaches, marshes, mangroves, cliffs, rocky reefs, and myriad offshore islands as well as an inland array of lakes, ponds, and wetlands are nesting grounds, feeding stops, and wintering areas for migrants as well as year-round habitats for millions of nonmigratory waterbirds.

The migration hot spots on these maps locate many of the most important nesting, wintering, refueling, and molting areas for waterbirds along the Pacific Flyway. Continued stewardship and enhanced protection of these sites are crucial to the well-being of millions of migratory and nonmigratory waterbirds. Most of the mapped sites shown are included in the Western Hemisphere Shorebird Reserve Network, a coordinated international effort to protect migratory shorebirds and their habitats.

1 Wrangel Island (Russia): This Russian Arctic island outpost supports nesting populations of thousands of snow geese, brant, sandhill cranes, red knots, and other waterbirds that winter in southern latitudes of the Pacific Flyway.

2 Izembek Lagoon (Alaska): Izembek National Wildlife Refuge is one of the most important waterfowl and shorebird breeding and staging habitats in the world. The site is especially important for waterfowl species (particularly geese) that undertake transoceanic flights as they move between breeding habitats in the Arctic and wintering habitats along the Pacific Flyway.

3 National Petroleum Reserve (Alaska): Located on the western North Slope of Alaska, this reserve encompasses a magnificent wilderness—larger than the state of Maine. It hosts the highest density of shorebirds in the circumpolar Arctic and provides critical nesting habitat for waterfowl, loons, grebes, gulls, terns, and jaegers. Hundreds of brant and white-fronted geese stop at Teshekpuk Lake while undergoing post-breeding wing molt prior to the fall migration.

Wrangel Island (Russia)

Greater white-fronted goose near its tundra nest site (Nunavut, Canada)

Izembek Lagoon (Alaska)

4 Arctic National Wildlife Refuge (Alaska): This large pristine refuge, which is threatened by proposed oil and gas developments, provides nesting habitat for extensive populations of migratory waterbirds, some of which migrate as far as Tierra del Fuego.

5 Mackenzie River Delta (Yukon, Northwest Territories): The Mackenzie River is one of the most important freshwater river systems in the world. At least two dozen species of migratory waterbirds rely on this watershed, including sandhill cranes, shorebirds, and many species of ducks. Islands in the outer delta support many thousands of nesting waterbirds that rely on this watershed and serve as important late-summer staging grounds for geese and tundra swans.

6 Banks Island (Northwest Territories, Beaufort Sea): The fourth-largest and westernmost island of the Canadian Arctic Archipelago, Banks Island provides nesting and feeding habitat for about 25,000 snow geese, a few thousand brant, as well as hundreds of Pacific loons, red-throated loons, glaucous gulls, red phalaropes, and many other shorebirds in two large migratory bird sanctuaries centered on the Egg and Thomsen Rivers.

Arctic National Wildlife Refuge (Alaska)

Mackenzie River Delta (Yukon, Northwest Territories)

Whimbrel parent and chick on the tundra (Alaska)

11

7 Pribilof Islands (Alaska): These remote islands in the Bering Sea are included in the Alaska Maritime National Wildlife Refuge. The islands are home to at least 2 million nesting seabirds, including murres, auklets, puffins, and most of the world's population of red-legged kittiwakes.

8 Yukon Delta National Wildlife Refuge (Alaska): This refuge encompasses about 19 million acres and is the second-largest refuge in the US. It provides nesting habitat for one of the world's largest aggregations of waterbirds, including roughly 500,000 shorebirds, over a million ducks, hundreds of thousands of geese and swans, and tens of thousands of loons, grebes, and sandhill cranes.

9 Kachemak Bay (Alaska): Each spring the extensive intertidal areas along Homer Spit attract over 100,000 shorebirds representing twenty-five different species, the most numerous of which are western sandpipers, dunlins, and dowitchers.

10 Copper River Delta (Alaska): This vast estuary ecosystem is nourished by six glacial river systems that arise in the Chugach Mountains. More than a million shorebirds can be found on the delta from late April to mid-May, and concentrations of more than 200,000 shorebirds per square mile have been reported during the peak period of spring migration.

Pribilof Islands (Alaska)

King eider (male) on a tundra pond (Alaska)

Yukon Delta National Wildlife Refuge (Alaska)

11 Stikine River Delta (Alaska): Diverse delta habitats support millions of migrating shorebirds, thousands of waterfowl and sandhill cranes, and spectacular concentrations of bald eagles. This is an important feeding stopover for sandpipers migrating between southern wintering grounds and nesting areas in Arctic Alaska.

12 Fraser River Estuary (British Columbia): Hundreds of thousands of migrating shorebirds pass through this area each year, and tens of thousands overwinter. On a single day in spring, the mudflats of Roberts Bank may abound with over 100,000 western sandpipers.

13 Grays Harbor Estuary (Washington): Each spring and fall, more than half a million shorebirds use Grays Harbor National Wildlife Refuge and adjacent intertidal habitats. It is an important feeding stop for red knots migrating north in spring.

14 Willapa Bay and Long Beach Peninsula (Washington): President Franklin Roosevelt established the Willapa Bay National Wildlife Refuge in 1937 to protect migrating and wintering populations of brant, ducks, and shorebirds.

Grays Harbor Estuary (Washington)

Two male hooded mergansers in a territorial face-off (British Columbia, Canada)

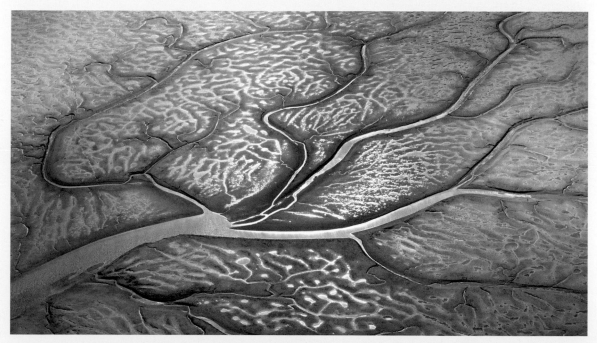

Willapa Bay and Long Beach Peninsula (Washington)

13

15 Klamath Basin (Oregon, California): Historically, the basin supported some of the largest concentrations of migrating waterfowl in North America. Populations plummeted after extensive loss of wetlands due to agricultural development. Water availability continues to be a major problem.

16 Humboldt Bay National Wildlife Refuge (California): The bays, mudflats, wetlands, dunes, and agricultural fields of this refuge support hundreds of thousands of migrating shorebirds and waterfowl as well as a rich assortment of overwintering birds.

17 Sacramento Valley (California): Valley wetlands are one of the world's premier wintering areas for ducks, geese, and swans. In spring and fall the area hosts hundreds of thousands of migrating shorebirds.

18 San Francisco Bay (California): The bay is important for vast numbers of migrating and wintering shorebirds, as well as for significant breeding populations of snowy plovers, American avocets, and black-necked stilts.

19 The Grasslands (California): In spring the San Joaquin Valley wetlands, riparian areas, scrublands, and pastoral lands attract multitudes of migrating shorebirds, where many of these birds spend the winter.

20 Lahontan Valley Wetlands (Nevada): In years with good precipitation, these wetlands abound with life, including hundreds of thousands of shorebirds.

Klamath Basin (Oregon, California)

San Francisco Bay (California)

14

21 Mono Lake (California): The lake's teeming populations of brine shrimp and alkali flies nourish up to a million shorebirds, grebes, gulls, ducks, and geese, including vast numbers of phalaropes (Wilson's and red-necked), hundreds of thousands of eared grebes, and more than thirty other waterbird species.

22 Owens Lake (California): Dust mitigation measures have created habitats that attract many shorebirds, including concentrations of American avocets, least sandpipers, and snowy plovers.

23 Great Salt Lake (Utah): Huge populations of brine shrimp and brine flies provide essential food resources for millions of eared grebes and more than a million shorebirds, sometimes including huge numbers of Wilson's phalaropes.

Mono Lake (California)

Snowy plover foraging for flies at Point Reyes National Seashore (California)

Great Salt Lake (Utah)

24 Alto Golfo de California y Delta del Río Colorado (Sonora, Baja California): The upper gulf and river delta are magnets for large numbers of shorebirds, including more than one-third of the Pacific population of red knots.

25 Golfo de Santa Clara (Sonora): Gulf beaches host spawning gulf grunion, whose eggs are an important food source for red knots migrating northward in March and April.

26 Complejo Lagunar Ojo de Liebre–Guerrero Negro (Baja California Sur): The lagoon complex, well known as a birthing area for gray whales, supports large numbers of brant and a diverse assortment of shorebirds, especially marbled godwits, red knots, and short-billed dowitchers.

27 Complejo San Ignacio (Baja California Sur): The lagoons of this complex—another birthing area for gray whales—attract an abundance of brant, marbled godwits, and snowy plovers, as well as many other shorebird species.

Alto Golfo de California y Delta del Río Colorado (Sonora, Baja California)

White-faced ibis heading north across the Gulf of California (Mexico)

Complejo San Ignacio (Baja California Sur)

28 Bahía de Tóbari (Sonora): A rich diversity of shorebirds has been found here in early winter, including substantial populations of American avocets, willets, and marbled godwits.

29 Bahía de Santa María (Sinaloa): Mangroves, marshes, and dunes support major concentrations of migratory and resident waterbirds.

30 Ensenada de Pabellones (Sinaloa): Coastal habitats sustain western sandpipers, marbled godwits, and American avocets, as part of an assemblage of hundreds of thousands of wintering shorebirds.

31 Marismas Nacionales (Nayarit): The area's lagoons and wetlands host an abundance of shorebirds representing more than three dozen species, including large numbers of American avocets.

CENTRAL AMERICA

32 Delta del Estero Real (Nicaragua): The delta's mudflats, marshes, and mangroves attract large numbers of Wilson's plovers, whimbrels, semipalmated sandpipers, and other waterbirds.

33 Parte Alta de la Bahía de Panama (Panama): More than a million shorebirds migrate through this area of mangrove-bordered mudflats. Hundreds of thousands of western and semipalmated sandpipers sometimes assemble on the tidal flats in spring.

Marismas Nacionales (Nayarit)

Parte Alta de la Bahía de Panama (Panama)

34 Delta del Río Iscuandé (Colombia): This area supports significant populations of Wilson's plovers, spotted sandpipers, whimbrels, and many other shorebirds.

35 Lagunas de Ecuasal (Ecuador): Salt evaporation ponds serve as an important habitat for migrating Wilson's phalarope.

36 Manglares de San Pedro de Vice (Peru): This habitat is important for sanderlings and two dozen other shorebird species.

37 Estuario de Virrilá (Peru): The estuary attracts many shorebirds, including large numbers of snowy plovers, whimbrels, and sanderlings.

38 Reserva Nacional de Paracas (Peru): Several thousand sanderlings and large numbers of other migratory shorebirds frequent the beaches and rocky shores of this reserve.

39 Humedal del Río Lluta (Chile): Migratory whimbrels and sanderlings, as well as South American endemic species, are among the numerous shorebirds that use this wetland.

40 Monumento Natural Laguna de los Pozuelos (Argentina): This Andean wetland is used by more than 100,000 shorebirds each year, including many Baird's sandpipers and Wilson's phalaropes.

41 Laguna Mar Chiquita (Argentina): Hundreds of thousands of Wilson's phalaropes sometimes winter in this large saline lake in the company of big flocks of flamingos.

Reserva Nacional de Paracas (Peru)

Laguna Mar Chiquita (Argentina)

42 Desembocadura y Estuario del Río Maipo (Chile): River-mouth waters, wetlands, and beaches host substantial populations of whimbrels, American oystercatchers, and other waterbirds.

43 Humedales de Maullín (Chile): This wetland complex is important habitat for Hudsonian godwits.

44 Humedales Orientales de Chiloé (Chile): Chiloé's shores and wetlands provide crucial winter habitat for long-distance migratory populations of Hudsonian godwits and whimbrels. Most shorebird habitats intermingle with aquaculture and receive intensive consumptive use by people.

45 Estuario del Río Gallegos (Argentina): The estuary's tidal mudflats and marshes annually support large flocks of shorebirds, including long-distance migrants that nest in Arctic North America.

46 Bahía Lomas (Chile): The bay's tidal flats and marshes are important wintering areas for red knots, Hudsonian godwits, and other long-distance migrants.

47 Costa Atlántica de Tierra del Fuego (Argentina): This remote coastal area supports large numbers of long-distance migratory Hudsonian godwits, red knots, and white-rumped sandpipers, as well as other waterbirds that nest in southern South America.

Humedales Orientales de Chiloé (Chile)

Bahía Lomas (Chile)

White-rumped sandpiper preening its feathers (Argentina)

19

CHAPTER 2

Fueling the Journey

The coast is an edgy place. Living on the coast presents certain stark realities and a wild, bare beauty. Continent confronts ocean. Weather intensifies. It's a place of tide and tantrum; of flirtations among fresh- and saltwaters, forests and shores; of tense negotiations with an ocean that gives much but demands more.

—Carl Safina, *The View from Lazy Point: A Natural Year in an Unnatural World*

The wild edge between land and sea—where "continent confronts ocean"—sets a dramatic stage for the migratory waterbirds that travel the Pacific Americas Flyway. The shallow bays, rocky shorelines, tide pools, mudflats, sandy beaches, and estuary wetlands offer a lavish seaside smorgasbord that suits every diet and foraging behavior. Inland of this coastal foraging corridor, a mosaic of freshwater lakes, ponds, rivers, and marshy wetlands, and dryland habitats, add to the bounty of food resources available for overland migrations.

Migratory waterbirds face a daunting spectrum of energy challenges as they embark on their epic journeys—a high-intensity endurance test by any measure. Consider the food needs of Arctic terns, one of the world's most famous long-distance migrants, departing on a 12,500-mile (20,000-km) flight from Alaska to the southern polar seas. Migrating western sandpipers often fly a couple hundred miles (few hundred km), or sometimes more than 1,400 miles (2,200 km), before stopping to refuel at one of several key sites. For resting and refueling, these sandpipers rely on several mudflat foraging areas in North and Central America, including the Copper River and Stikine River Deltas in Alaska, the Fraser River Estuary in British Columbia, and the upper Bay of Panama. How do these small migrants power flights across such vast distances?

Arctic tern

In contrast to the periodic fueling stops of western sandpipers, Alaska-nesting Pacific golden plovers are powered solely by energy stores accumulated by gorging on tiny invertebrates and small fruits prior to embarking on nonstop flights of more than 5,000 miles (8,000 km) to their wintering areas in Hawaii, American Samoa, Fiji, or other islands in the southwestern Pacific Ocean. Some golden plovers return to Alaska by way of eastern Asia, but their clockwise migration path is often more irregular than in this simplified example because of shifting winds and other weather factors.

ALASKA
Breeding

JAPAN
Feeding

AMERICAN SAMOA
Boreal winter

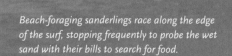

Beach-foraging sanderlings race along the edge of the surf, stopping frequently to probe the wet sand with their bills to search for food.

After feasting on brine shrimp before migration, some adult Wilson's phalaropes—with fat loads sometimes exceeding one-half of their body weight—temporarily become too heavy to fly.

THE ADVANTAGES OF BEING FAT

The most critical task for all migratory waterbirds is finding sufficient food to fuel the energetically costly journeys between their breeding and nonbreeding areas. Given their high metabolic rates and airborne lifestyles, birds must accumulate substantial energy reserves before they begin migration, locate good foraging areas along the way for refueling, or strike a balance between these two strategies to meet their energetic requirements for the full journey.

Fat—"high-octane" biofuel that migrants amass in great quantities—yields twice as much energy per ounce (gram) than either protein or carbohydrate. A bird's fat reserves appear as yellowish deposits under the skin in various parts of the body. When "burned" as fuel, fat yields water as a by-product, which is crucial in preventing dehydration during a long flight.

Long-distance migrants need enormous reserves of fat to complete their epic journeys. For them, obesity is a necessity. Just before migrating, transoceanic migrants feed ravenously and put on body fat amounting to one-third to one-half of their total body weight. Bristle-thighed curlews start out with fat loads averaging 42 percent of their body weight and make trans-Pacific flights of 2,500 to 6,200 miles (4,000 to 10,000 km) or more as they migrate between staging areas in Alaska and wintering sites on islands in the central and southern Pacific Ocean. A remarkable ability to quickly process and make use of stored fats allows some migrants to fly nonstop for thousands of miles.

Bar-tailed godwits are legendary for nonstop transoceanic marathons that rely solely on body energy stores. Before the advent of modern tracking technology, researchers assumed that these large shorebirds used islands along their flight path as stepping-stones for resting and refueling between their breeding grounds in Arctic Alaska and wintering areas in New Zealand. Satellite tracking has shown that the godwits complete most of their annual migrations of more than 17,500 miles (28,500 km) between New Zealand and Alaska as a few nonstop flights of several thousand miles.

Like professional athletes, long-distance migrants undergo highly sophisticated preparations to maximize strength and endurance. A key issue for these migrants is balancing fat stores against flight efficiency. Prior to migration, most migrants boost their flight performance by increasing the size of their flight muscles and enhancing heart-lung function. Simultaneous increases in the size of their gizzard, stomach, intestine, and liver facilitate rapid fueling and digestion. In some species these organs shrink as migration time approaches, eliminating unnecessary weight during the flight. While the birds are airborne on nonstop long-haul flights, their internal systems shift to a cruising gear that maximizes fuel efficiency.

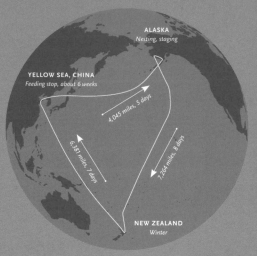

ALASKA
Nesting, staging

YELLOW SEA, CHINA
Feeding stop, about 6 weeks

4,045 miles, 5 days

6,381 miles, 7 days

7,264 miles, 8 days

NEW ZEALAND
Winter

A bar-tailed godwit departing from Alaska to New Zealand carries less than 0.5 pounds (0.23 kg) of fat, but this is sufficient for a 7,264-mile (11,700-km) nonstop flight lasting more than a week! Juvenile bar-tailed godwits begin their migration marathon with fat loads of up to 55 percent of their body weight. A Boeing 737-700 jet aircraft with full tanks carries about 45,500 pounds (20,400 kg) of fuel, has a range of about 3,500 miles (5,630 km), and burns 5,000 to 6,000 pounds (2,270 to 2,720 kg) of fuel per hour.

Understanding the ocean's central role in fueling the epic journeys of millions of migratory waterbirds begins with the miniature world of "ocean drifters," or plankton, which comprise two major groups—phytoplankton and zooplankton. Phytoplankton are the microscopic plantlike organisms—primarily diatoms, dinoflagellates, coccolithophores, and cyanobacteria—that thrive in the sea's sunlit surface waters. These single-celled organisms contain chlorophyll and harvest energy from the sun through the process of photosynthesis, transforming water, carbon dioxide, and minerals into atmospheric oxygen and the incredible array of organic compounds required for life on the earth.

Phytoplankton are the solar-powered engine that sustains the amazing biodiversity of ocean life. By providing the basic building blocks of life (protein, fat, and carbohydrates), phytoplankton are as crucial to the survival of the billions of migratory waterbirds that travel the world's flyways as they are, ultimately, to all life-forms on our planet, including us.

Looking at a drop of seawater through a microscope is an amazing experience, akin to viewing the nighttime sky with a telescope. But in seawater, the equivalent "Milky Way" is alive—pulsating, eating, being devoured, and reproducing before our eyes—a startling microcosm of strange-looking life-forms known collectively as plankton.

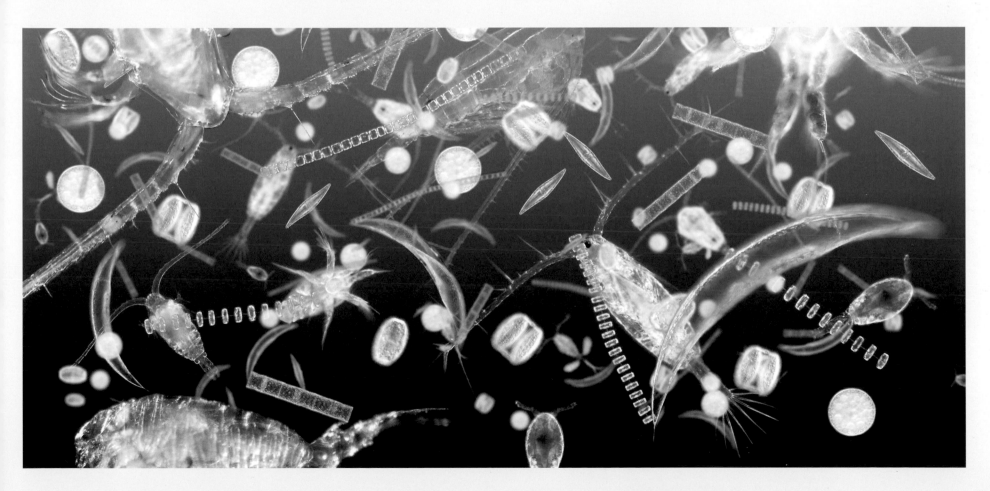

Phytoplankton "blooms" in oceans and estuaries attract enormous swarms of tiny animals known collectively as zooplankton—copepods, krill, and other small crustaceans, jellies, and the larval stages of many kinds of invertebrates and fishes. Some zooplankton are readily recognizable as shrimplike, but many are bizarre spiny or big-eyed forms that defy identification except by specialists. Zooplankton are a rich source of energy and nutrients—directly or indirectly—for a broad spectrum of life-forms, ranging from other zooplankton (big ones eat smaller ones) and fishes to waterbirds, whales, and humans.

The sea's seductive aroma is produced, in part, as a natural side effect of the death (senescence) of phytoplankton when a prolific "bloom" of these microalgal organisms exhausts the available nutrient supply or when they are grazed on by zooplankton. The bacterial decomposition of microalgae releases several volatile chemical compounds, one of which is the sulfur-rich gas dimethyl sulphide (DMS). Wave action often whips this gelatinous algal "broth" into the sparkling white, DMS-enriched drifts of foam delivered to the shoreline by the tides.

Phytoplankton blooms with high concentrations of certain types of dinoflagellates give off a bluish-green bioluminescence at night when agitated by a diving seabird foraging on zooplankton, a swimming fish, waves along a beach, or a boat's wake.

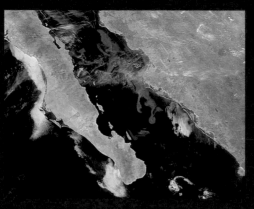

This NASA satellite photograph shows a jade-green phyto-plankton bloom in the Gulf of California associated with an upwelling zone along the western edge of the Mexican mainland. The pink cloud of krill (shrimplike crustaceans) is being fed on by an enormous school of Pacific sardines.

Once decimated by overfishing in more northerly waters, Pacific sardines continue to be seasonally abundant off the west coast of Mexico's Baja Peninsula and in the Midriff Island area of the Gulf of California (Sea of Cortez). Sardines, traveling in schools that contain hundreds of thousands to millions of individuals, are a seasonal mainstay in the diets of vast numbers of migratory waterbirds, including Heermann's gulls and elegant terns. Each year, about 500,000 gulls and terns nest on Isla Rasa in the central Gulf of California, consuming an estimated 65 tons of sardines daily.

Krill—shrimplike crustaceans that feed on phytoplankton—nourish schooling fishes, such as these Pacific sardines near Baja California, as well as millions of seabirds.

MARINE PRODUCTIVITY
HOT SPOTS

As late winter transitions into spring along the Pacific coast of North America, high-pressure weather systems bring fair weather and strong winds out of the west and northwest. Vibrant interactions of these springtime winds, Earth's rotation, and the southward flow of the California Current push coastal surface waters seaward and generate an upwelling of cool nutrient-laden waters from the seafloor to shallower depths where sunlight penetrates. A similar upwelling process operates along the north-flowing Humboldt Current along the west coast of South America.

With spring's arrival, the ocean awakens in a prodigious flourishing of life. The nutrient-replenished waters in the sunlit upwelling zone stimulate a proliferation of phytoplankton that, in turn, results in a population boom of zooplankton. Similar bursts of productivity also occur in more localized areas along the coast and in connected straits wherever waters flow across submerged banks, submarine canyons, or seamounts and where rivers deliver a bounty of nutrients carried from inland watersheds.

Millions of seabirds depend on these fertile coastal waters and their rich plankton and fish populations to feed themselves and their offspring and to fuel their wide-ranging travels. Phytoplankton blooms often create vast swirls of color—red, teal blue, turquoise, and green—that are mostly associated with dense concentrations of different species of light-reflecting phytoplankton. What isn't visible is the scent-rich slick of concentrated DMS that persists on the sea surface in the wake of a bloom. For tubenose seabirds such as albatrosses or shearwaters, the "freshly opened oyster" aroma of DMS signals a banquet, and the diners waste no time in following the "scent trail." Tubenose seabirds are not the only beneficiaries of these offshore bonanzas, which also attract gulls, kittiwakes, scoters, loons, grebes, murres, auklets, puffins, and seafaring shorebirds such as phalaropes.

A humpback whale joins a feeding frenzy of thousands of shearwaters at an upwelling hot spot in the Alaska Current just off the coast of southeast Alaska, where the sunset special is a two-for-one dinner of krill and tiny fish. Concentrated patches of krill can give the ocean an orange-red hue. Near Chile's Chiloé Island in 1835, Charles Darwin saw immense flocks of sooty shearwaters settle on waters "coloured by clouds of small crustacea."

Tubenose seabirds such as this Laysan albatross use their finely tuned sense of smell to locate swarms of krill and other patches of food scattered across the vast ocean.

The marine feast that supports seabirds along the Pacific coast is not always dependable. During El Niño events, every two to seven years, warmer than average sea temperatures dominate the central and eastern tropical Pacific Ocean, which affects weather patterns and ocean conditions across a vast area. One effect is a slowing or halting of coastal upwelling processes that deliver cool nutrient-rich water to the upper water layers where most seabirds forage. Under these conditions, phytoplankton production is greatly diminished, and the resulting food shortages affect the entire marine ecosystem.

Over the past decade major episodes of ocean warming—marine heat waves—and associated reductions in food quantity and quality have resulted in unprecedented seabird mortality along the Pacific coast of North America. Since the mid-2010s, vast numbers of murres and other seabirds have starved to death and washed up on shores throughout coastal Alaska because of severe food shortages caused by the warming of ocean waters. Once-thriving murre colonies now appear deserted in several areas. Similar catastrophes have struck the coast farther south. Between British Columbia and California an estimated 250,000 to 500,000 Cassin's auklets died of starvation during the winter of 2014–2015.

Sooty shearwaters converge in a feeding frenzy in Monterey Bay, California.

HARMFUL ALGAL BLOOMS

Although "normal" phytoplankton blooms remain a key component of the marine food web, harmful algal blooms have become an increasingly common phenomenon worldwide. Over the past several decades, toxic algal blooms, often referred to as "red tides," were identified as the cause of mass mortality events affecting shellfish, fish, seabirds, and marine mammals along both shorelines of the Americas. The deadliest of these toxic blooms are often associated with dense concentrations of neurotoxin-rich species of dinoflagellates and diatoms. Plankton-eating clams, mussels, or fishes may accumulate these neurotoxins without ill effect, but the consumption of these tainted fish or shellfish can sicken or kill the animals that eat them, including us.

Not all harmful algal blooms involve toxins. In the largest marine bird mortality event ever reported, an estimated 10,500 carcasses of surf scoters, white-winged scoters, and common murres washed ashore along the Washington coast in September and October 2009. The massive die-off occurred during a phytoplankton bloom of a single species of dinoflagellate that coincided with a large aggregation of vulnerable marine birds undergoing premigratory molt in a traditional staging area along the coast. The birds died not from ingesting a toxin, but rather from the effects of the surfactant-rich foam produced by the bacterial decomposition of billions of these tiny organisms. The surfactant destroyed the waterproofing oils that waterbirds typically preen into their feathers to keep their bodies warm and dry.

Among the bountiful populations of marine wildlife along the coast of North America are small schooling fish—sand lance, surf smelt, northern anchovy, and Pacific herring. All are incredibly important food resources for waterbirds in coastal waters. Herring are particularly important during their spawning season, which begins in autumn and winter in California and gradually spreads northward until it reaches Alaska in summer. Vast schools of spawning males release white clouds of sperm in shallow water as the females deposit enormous numbers of sticky eggs that cling to plants and rocks. Soon the seascape gleams with sparkling pearl-like eggs immersed in milky water.

The great wave of spawning herring attracts a frenzy of tens of thousands of seabirds, ducks, and shorebirds gorging on the succulent eggs or on the fish. Flocks of scoters and harlequin ducks follow the waves of spawning herring northward and feast on the eggs before departing for breeding grounds to the north or inland. Northward-migrating flocks of brant, which usually stick to a salad-bar diet of eelgrass and sea lettuce (a green algae) add a fat-rich side order of herring eggs whenever they have the opportunity. Nonmigratory birds also take advantage of the reproductive explosion of herring. On some days in the Salish Sea, nearly the entire local population of screaming glaucous-winged gulls descends on the herring spawning waters.

Top: A silver wave of spawning Pacific herring sweeps northward along the Pacific coastline in early spring each year, providing succulent meals for hungry waterbirds preparing to migrate. This aerial photo shows a spawning area near Sitka, Alaska, where the ocean is milky from the vast quantity of eggs and milt.

Bottom: A glaucous-winged gull and the catch of the day—herring.

Facing page: In spring, surf scoters gather by the thousands to feed on herring eggs in the intertidal zone in Berners Bay in southeast Alaska.

Far to the south another kind of silver wave hits the beaches of northwestern Mexico. In spring, when lunar cycles trigger the season's highest tides, the stage is set for an unusual beach party—the amazing spawning ritual of the gulf grunion, a tiny fish related to sardines. Unlike California grunion, which swarm moonlit beaches along the southern California coastline, gulf grunion spawn day or night, depending on the tides, and only in the northern Gulf of California. The annual mating dance takes place as fish thrash and squirm in the watery sand at the high-tide line. Females corkscrew backward into the sand and release their eggs in the curled embrace of a sperm-releasing male. Then it's back to the sea—if the little fishes can evade the gauntlet of ravenous gulls and pelicans.

Meanwhile, the grunion orgy has attracted other hungry birds: flocks of chunky salmon-breasted sandpipers—red knots in their breeding finery. The red knots in the upper Gulf of California will soon be heading to their Arctic nesting grounds in northwestern Alaska or as far as Russia's Wrangel Island—worlds apart from this sun-washed Sonoran Desert seascape. The feast of energy-rich grunion eggs gets the red knots started on their long journey but does not sustain them the whole way. Farther north, along the coast of Washington, knots switch their diet to take advantage of abundant populations of small clams, a diet that also sustains them in winter in the lagoons of Pacific coastal Baja California and in many places along their migration routes.

Pacific sardine populations continue to be seasonally abundant off the west coast of Mexico's Baja Peninsula and in the Gulf of California. Schools of sardines often contain hundreds of thousands of fish and are a seasonal mainstay in the diets of many seabirds. Each year about 500,000 Heermann's gulls and elegant terns nest on Isla Rasa in the central Gulf of California, consuming an estimated 65 tons of sardines daily.

A feast of gulf grunion eggs fuels the journeys of red knots migrating north from the Gulf of California.

Red knots

GRAZING THE GREEN WAVE

With spring's arrival the days grow longer and warmer along the Pacific coast, and the pulse of life quickens. On land, in shallow bays and estuaries, and across myriad lakes, ponds, and inland wetlands, an emerald flush of new leaves and sprouts spreads northward. By early February millions of plant-grazing waterfowl—geese, swans, and dabbling ducks—head north, grazing the green wave as they make their way to their breeding grounds.

Along the Pacific Flyway another type of green wave takes over at the ocean's edge: underwater meadows of eelgrass. This marine flowering plant grows in submerged intertidal habitats and blooms underwater. Extremely fast-growing, a single acre of eelgrass produces almost 10 tons of leaves annually—a rate of productivity rivaling that of tropical rain forests. On a warm, sunny day if you were to lower a hydrophone into a bed of eelgrass, you might be surprised to hear the champagne-like fizz emanating from the plant as its leaves absorb carbon dioxide and release oxygen.

On their wintering grounds and during migration, brant feed intensively on eelgrass and sea lettuce (a fast-growing, translucent green alga). Neither of these foods is particularly rich in nutrients, but they grow abundantly across an enormous area of the Pacific Flyway and so provide a dependable food resource for migrating brant. The green larder helps the birds arrive in their arctic and subarctic nesting grounds in good condition and ready to nest.

BRINE SHRIMP SPECIALISTS

At the end of the breeding season and under cover of darkness, a million or more eared grebes prepare to leave their nesting areas in freshwater wetlands in interior central North America to fly to California's Mono Lake or Utah's Great Salt Lake. The annual pilgrimage to these hypersaline lakes is a critical stage in the unique life history of grebes. For the next three to four months, adult grebes will gorge on the lakes' bounty of brine shrimp and brine flies, eventually doubling their weight with stored fat in preparation for a nonstop flight to overwintering areas primarily along the coast of Southern California and western Mexico. These same foods are also critical fuel sources for Wilson's phalaropes as they embark on long flights to South America.

Brine shrimp eggs and hatchling larvae

A Wilson's phalarope (above) is poised in midcapture mode while its flock mates settle down along the shores of Mono Lake. Mono Lake and Great Salt Lake are too salty to support fish, but they do provide eared grebes, Wilson's phalaropes, and other salt-tolerant migrants with prodigious quantities of brine shrimp and small flies. Brine shrimp make up about 90 percent of the eared grebe diet during their refueling stop at Mono Lake.

One of the most astonishing sources of food for migratory birds was discovered recently by biologists studying western sandpipers on the Salish Sea coast of British Columbia. These small birds—the most numerous shorebird along the west coast of North America—were thought to rely almost exclusively on small invertebrates (such as crustaceans, clams, snails, and marine worms) as their primary food. Diet analyses revealed that as much as half of the fat stored by the sandpipers was derived from biofilm, a mélange of bacteria, protozoa, algae, and diatoms that grows on the surface of tidal mudflats. The biofilm "frosting" on mudflats is extremely nutritious, serving as a rich source of energy and omega-3 fatty acids that may be vital during migration.

Estuary mudflats appear to provide the perfect conditions for the development of biofilm. On the Fraser River Estuary, biofilm is heavily grazed by western sandpipers on their northward migration. The sandpipers also graze biofilm during the southward migration in late summer, although in smaller quantities in relation to invertebrate prey. Biofilm grazing by shorebirds likely occurs on estuary mudflats worldwide.

Western sandpipers and other shorebirds have a fringe on the tongue that allows them to lap up biofilm, a predictable and prolific food resource.

CHAPTER 3

Wings on the Wind

Winging westward, it climbs
each step up to the naked blue:
the entire sky is its tower,
and the world is cleansed by its movement.

—Pablo Neruda, *Art of Birds*

A royal tern emerges from the sea after a plunge-dive in pursuit of fish.

...en compare birds to airplanes and use aeronautical terms to describe the mechanics of flight, but bird wings are superior to aircraft wings in many ways. Bird wings can incur significant damage, including lost or broken feathers, and still provide safe flight, and birds have the remarkable ability to "repair" their wings through feather replacement. Bird wings can instantaneously change shape and orientation for split-second maneuverability and speed changes. When folded up, a bird's wings are held close to the body to protect vital parts from cold, rain, and injury. Aircraft engineers are still struggling to catch up with 150 million years of bird-wing evolution that has produced more than 10,000 models that are still in the air!

...nation.
...nation of
...d's energy and
...span continents and
...wide arc of the Pacific
...ut strong, feathers give birds a
...he skies.

Long-distance...
have long pointe...
minimal drag. Du...
up to thirty years, a...
750,000 miles (1.2 m...

A bird's main flight feathers consist of two types: primaries and secondaries. The primary feathers, as shown on the outstretched wings of this common loon, are on the outer half of the wing and are generally longer than the secondaries and asymmetrical; and each one is independently adjustable to allow maximum flight control. The secondaries are on the inner half of the wing, closest to the body, and tend to be shorter and broader than the primaries, with blunter ends. Contour feathers cover most of the body and give the bird its aerodynamic shape, providing warmth and protection.

A SUITE OF SPECIALIZATIONS

Since their earliest glimmerings in dinosaurs about 250 million years ago, feathers have evolved into one of nature's most powerful and beautiful adornments. Feathered flight evolved in concert with a suite of anatomical and physiological specializations that helped birds colonize the far corners of the globe—reductions in body weight suited to an airborne existence, an exquisite feathered cloak that both insulates and streamlines the body, and enhancements in the power and endurance needed for long-distance flight.

Loons are divers par excellence. Their sleek heavy body and large webbed feet enable them to submerge powerfully and make quick maneuvers in pursuit of prey. Most dives last less than a minute, but loons can remain underwater for three minutes or longer.

All birds devote a considerable amount of time each day to feather maintenance. In addition to taking water or dust baths, birds use their bills to manipulate and preen their feathers, removing dirt and ectoparasites and realigning the feathers to preserve their functionality. Many species, especially waterbirds, use their bill to spread oily secretions from a gland at the base of the tail to maintain the water repellency of their feathers.

This pair of spectacled eiders, with the female on the nest and the male floating nearby, illustrate the beauty and functional utility of the female's camouflage plumage and the male's breeding season finery.

Brown pelicans are masterful plunge-divers for fish.

Harlequin ducks are unusual of among sea ducks, migrating inland to breed along fast-flowing rivers and streams and spending the winter months in the surf and intertidal zone along the Pacific coastline. Their ability to swim and forage in turbulent white water, diving to the bottom to pick larval invertebrates off rocky substates, is unmatched.

The airborne lifestyle of birds requires that they be light in weight yet strong, and their skeleton reflects these needs. With the exception of waterbirds whose bones are specialized for diving, the large bones are hollow but internally reinforced with struts—the natural model for human-designed trusses that provide lightweight structural support for buildings, bridges, and aircraft wings.

Key among the physiological adaptations that enhance the capacity of birds for long-distance flight is their impressive aerobic physiology, which includes exceptionally rapid transfer of the bird's internal energy resources to the flight muscles. Additionally, the respiratory system of birds features an unusual arrangement of air sacs and tubes that results in a one-way flow of air through the lungs—an extremely efficient system for delivering oxygen to the internal organs.

Mastery of the air by birds depends on the distinctive shape of their wings—thick and rounded in front, curved on the upper and lower surfaces, and tapered thin at the rear. Each feather-sculpted wing functions as a superb lift-generating airfoil—a design copied by aircraft engineers. Once the bird takes off, sustaining lift requires forward motion, or thrust, and this is largely achieved by wing flapping. Alterations in flapping rate and intricate adjustments in the position and angle of the wing and tail feathers allow birds to make extremely fast changes in speed and direction.

Above: Bird bills vary in size and shape according to the bird's diet and foraging behavior. The hooklike tip of the double-crested cormorant's bill is perfect for catching and holding its prey.

Right: Horned puffin emerges with a bill full of fish

Marine worms are a favorite food for many shorebirds, such as this sanderling, but extracting those worms from their burrows isn't easy. Many shorebirds have sensory organs near the bill tip that enable them to locate buried prey.

The wings of migratory birds come in many shapes and sizes. The exquisitely tapered wings of most long-distance migratory birds, such as terns and shorebirds, allow air to slip smoothly off the wing tip, reducing turbulence and improving flight efficiency. Some waterbirds, such as murres and puffins, have wings that work as well for aerial flight as they do for swimming or "flying" underwater in pursuit of food.

Some majestic soaring birds (sandhill cranes and bald eagles, for example) have big broad wings with rounded ends from which extend well-separated flexible primaries that reduce the higher level of turbulence and drag that would exist if the wings had blunt ends. This feature allows the birds to soar in slow circles on deflected updrafts along ridges and rising masses of warm air (thermals) from sun-warmed land. By gliding between updrafts and thermals, the birds can migrate across wide areas with minimal energy expenditure. Large expanses of water do not generate high-rising updrafts, so broad-winged soaring birds tend to avoid long passages over open water.

If broad wings are designed for soaring, how do black-footed and Laysan albatrosses—heavy birds weighing around 7 pounds (3.2 kg), about the same as a sandhill crane—soar for hours on end with narrow, tapered wings? The answer is that despite high wing loading, albatross wings have a lot of area relative to the wing tip (where most turbulence is generated), and it turns out that most of the lift in a wing is generated near the leading edge, so narrow albatross wings have a favorable lift-to-drag ratio. Albatross wings work best where wind speed is consistently high, so they rarely leave the windswept open ocean.

The broad wings of sandhill cranes allow easy soaring on updrafts. Sometimes the birds gain thousands of feet of altitude without flapping.

Albatrosses generally stay within about 50 feet (15.25 m) of the ocean surface, soaring on low updrafts deflected by waves and swells. To attain enough lift to take off from water or land, they run fast into a headwind while shallowly flapping their wings.

Barrow's goldeneye

TEAMWORK ALOFT

The iconic image of migration is a great V formation of geese coursing overhead. These flight formations—seen in large broad-winged birds that migrate in flocks, notably geese and sandhill cranes—arise when the birds take advantage of a peculiarity of aerodynamics to increase flight efficiency. The familiar V and diagonal formations of these birds come about as the birds adjust to their immediate wind conditions. At a bird's wing tip, air tends to move from below the wing (area of high pressure) to above it (low pressure). Most of this air swirls off behind the wing as a trailing whirlwind.

A bird flying diagonally behind and slightly above another bird can use these air swirls to optimize its lift-to-drag ratio—in other words, to increase its flight efficiency, and sometimes the trailing bird coordinates its wingbeats with the individual ahead of it in order to maximize the benefit. Young birds master the intricacies of formation flying through a natural urge to follow their parents, watching the flight behavior of flock mates, and as they feel the effects of their position on how hard they must work in order to stay with the group.

WINDSURFING

Like all good seafarers and pilots, migratory birds must pay attention to the weather, particularly the wind. They may be masters of the air, but they often depend on air moving in the "proper" direction, so correct timing is essential for a successful flight. The western sandpiper provides an excellent example of the ways in which small migrants take advantage of favorable winds. Northbound western sandpiper flocks depart from South America in late winter and migrate up the Pacific coast to breeding grounds in western Alaska. In summer and early autumn the birds head south, many bypassing southeast Alaska to make landfall along the west coast of British Columbia and beyond. Some continue south along the coast while others cross the continent to arrive on beaches located anywhere from Texas to the Carolinas.

The timing of these flights coincides in spring with winds generated by weather cells in the Gulf of Alaska. These low-pressure cells create a counterclockwise vortex, drawing winds from the south up along the western coast of North America. These winds bring us

storms and wet weather, but for birds they signal an easy flight north on favorable tailwinds. Once underway, sandpipers may climb to altitudes of 3,000 feet (900 m) or more to find the steady tailwinds they need to hurtle them northward. One tracked sandpiper made the 1,850-mile (3,000-km) flight from San Francisco Bay to the Copper River Delta in forty-two hours, averaging 44 miles (70 km) per hour.

For their southbound journeys at the end of the breeding season, western sandpipers will rely once again on counterclockwise-rotating low-pressure systems, but this time the cell's center will be to the east—the perfect trajectory for the full-throttle tailwinds that will push the travelers in a south to southeasterly direction. Similarly, bar-tailed godwits embarking on flights from southern Alaska to islands in the South Pacific take advantage of the same weather cell conditions for favorable tailwinds needed to accelerate their journeys.

The brant in this classic V formation are optimizing their flight efficiency by flying diagonally behind and slightly above another goose.

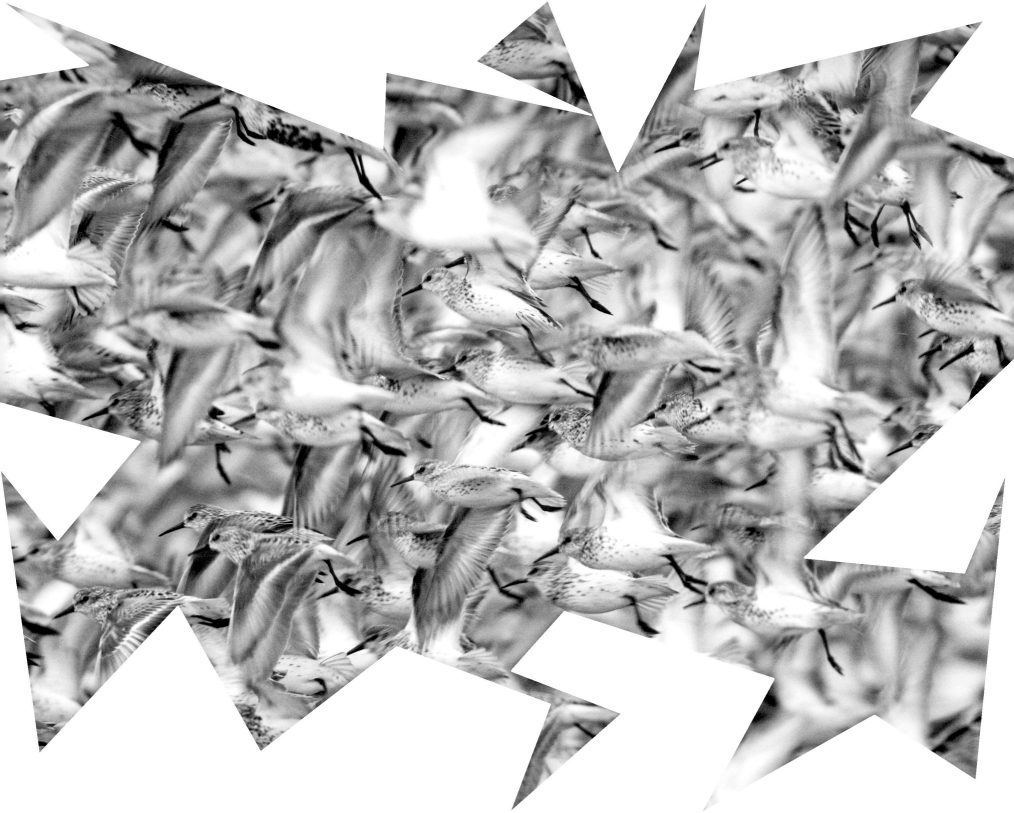

Facing page: Huge flocks of western sandpipers and dunlins head north to their Arctic breeding grounds in their spring plumage finery. Prior to embarking on the southbound migration, dunlin on or near their breeding grounds will have molted into their drab overwintering plumage prior to migration to the overwintering grounds.

This page: Tens of thousands of brant, as shown here, cackling geese, greater white-fronted geese, and snow geese fly to the Teshekpuk Lake area of the National Petroleum Reserve in northern Alaska to complete their premigratory molt, which renders them flightless and vulnerable. This globally important molting area is now threatened by proposed oil exploration and drilling.

COSTUME CHANGES

Feathers are incredibly durable, but they do wear out with continued exposure to the elements. Flight efficiency is of paramount importance to migratory birds, so feather replacement is crucial to their survival. Molting—the replacement of worn feathers with new ones—keeps birds in top flying condition. In most groups of birds, molt of the wing feathers is a gradual process requiring weeks to complete, with only one or a few flight feathers missing or growing at any one time, so the birds can still fly.

Growing feathers takes a lot of energy and nutrients, and flying with missing and growing feathers is hard work, so the molting process tends not to overlap with other demanding activities, such as nesting or migration. A few sandpiper species—dunlin, rock sandpiper, and Wilson's snipe, for example—molt on or near their nesting grounds and then head south with fresh plumage. Compare this process to that of some populations of black-bellied plover and Pacific golden plover, in which adults molt a few of their primaries and then suspend the process as they migrate to their nonbreeding areas, where they complete the molt.

The timing difference between molt and migration reaches a pinnacle in certain heavy-bodied waterbirds. For example, adult loons molt all their wing feathers simultaneously and become flightless for a few weeks in fall (red-throated loon) or winter through early spring (other loons). The loons molt in their coastal nonbreeding habitats, where the birds easily feed and rest without having to travel far, so being flightless for a while is not a problem. Waterfowl, too, become flightless for a few weeks while they simultaneously molt all their flight feathers. Many ducks and geese fly to specific areas to undergo this molt in safe places with plentiful food.

CHAPTER 4

Finding the Way

We humans get lost easily. . . .
The magnitude of
birds' migratory performances
staggers our imagination,
in terms of both physical exertion
and feats of navigation, because they are
vastly superior to anything we could,
as individuals, accomplish.

—Bernd Heinrich, *The Homing Instinct*

Migratory waterbirds navigate vast distances at sea and over land as if they had an onboard global positioning system—one that surpasses our high-tech devices by not needing batteries, charging devices, cellular towers, or satellites! In the not-so-distant past, most of what we knew about waterbird migration came from field surveys that recorded the locations of birds at different seasons and from the re-sightings or captures of birds that bore numbered tags or colored bands. Some intriguing data and tantalizing revelations emerged from these studies, but much of the time we simply watched the birds depart or arrive and puzzled over their origins, destinations, travel routes, and flight schedules.

Technological advancements in the 1940s provided a new tool—radar—that helped reveal some of the previously obscure aspects of bird migration. Weather radar can distinguish birds from rain and clearly shows the density of birds in the air and the direction they are moving. Radar is particularly illuminating because many birds migrate at night. Radar studies have helped us understand the factors that stimulate birds to begin their journeys as well as their seasonal and daily flight schedules.

Geolocators and other sophisticated miniature tracking devices are revolutionizing what we know about the travels of migratory birds.

Our understanding of the geographic and behavioral complexities of waterbird migration—the where and when—took a soaring leap forward over the past few decades. Migration scientists now have geolocators and an array of other sophisticated miniature tracking devices packed with complex electronics capable of recording a bird's specific location and aspects of its behavior and physiology as well as environmental data throughout the entire migratory journey. We've learned that the flight plans of these migrants are even more amazing than we previously imagined.

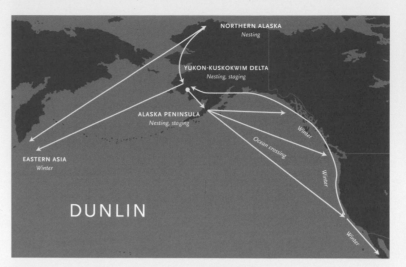

DUNLIN

Dunlins nesting in different parts of Alaska have astonishingly diverse migrations. Some dunlins nesting in northern Alaska winter in coastal eastern Asia, some stopping on the Yukon-Kuskokwim Delta (YKD) en route to Asia. Other populations nesting on the YKD and Alaska Peninsula winter mainly along the Pacific coast of North America.

A dunlin (breeding plumage) surveys the Alaska tundra for a suitable nesting spot.

THE HOMING INSTINCT

Each year, millions of waterbirds representing dozens of species migrate thousands of miles between their breeding and nonbreeding areas along the Pacific Flyway. These migrants exhibit an amazingly high degree of *site fidelity*, often traveling to the same spots where they nested, stopped to feed, or wintered in previous years. Many Alaska-nesting western sandpipers and semipalmated sandpipers return each year to the same stretch of beach at Costa del Este, Panama. Bar-tailed godwits provide an astonishing example of attachment to particular places. These large shorebirds make impressive multiday nonstop flights of several thousand miles when migrating over the Pacific Ocean between their nesting, feeding, and nonbreeding sites in Alaska, New Zealand, and the Yellow Sea in China. Most go to the same nesting, wintering, and feeding areas every year.

This pattern of annual reuse of specific sites along vast migration corridors is repeated by other trans-Pacific migrants such as bristle-thighed curlews and Pacific golden plovers, as well as by many other waterbird species that follow coastal or overland routes. The birds time their journeys with extraordinary precision and often successfully complete them despite challenging environmental conditions.

This female dunlin and her chick are enjoying a sunny day on the tundra near Barrow, Alaska.

The homing instinct is a compelling force in migratory birds. Field experiments have shown that even after being captured and moved to unfamiliar areas, experienced migratory birds are quickly able to adjust their course to arrive at their destination. Shearwaters, albatrosses, gulls, and terns that have been displaced hundreds or thousands of miles from their nesting areas often exhibit a strong determination to return home, seemingly driven by prior experience and familiarity. Knowing where to find food, shelter, and mating and nesting opportunities certainly improves a bird's chances of survival and successful reproduction. There are always some individuals—often juveniles—that explore new areas, and sometimes there is a payoff, such as the discovery of areas where severe storms have created new beaches or mudflats.

Cormorants also generally migrate during daylight hours and roost at night. Hundreds of migrating double-crested cormorants have been observed roosting in small groves of trees, for up to 15 hours or more on late fall nights.

Sandhill cranes normally migrate during daylight hours but sometimes they are observed migrating after dark, especially if they are nearing their migratory destination.

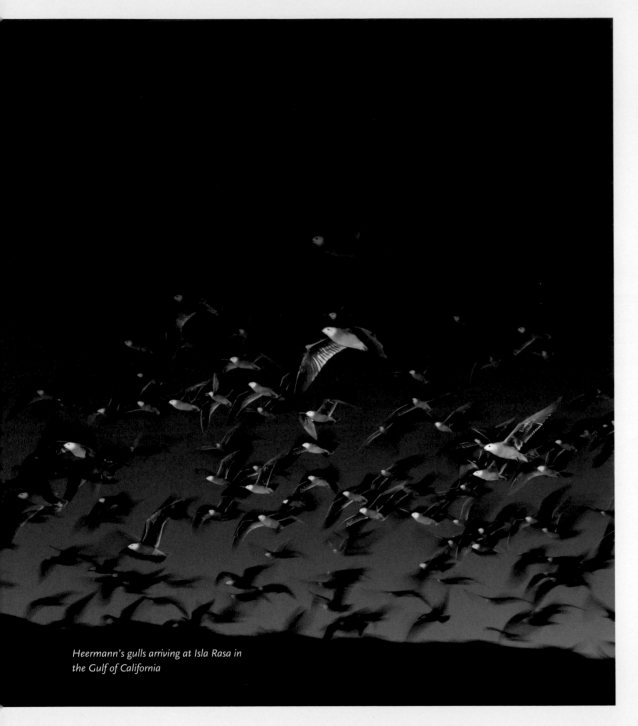

Heermann's gulls arriving at Isla Rasa in the Gulf of California

When migrants head to a distant destination, they determine their initial flight paths using an array of cues. Directional cues may include familiar topographic landmarks, such as coastlines and large mountain ranges. Birds also have instinctive responses to compass cues provided by the position and apparent movement of the sun, sunset light polarization patterns, stellar cues (stars in the night sky), or the earth's magnetic field (geomagnetism). Recent research suggests that birds have light-dependent magnetic detector molecules in their eyes and perceive geomagnetic direction as a visual cue. Birds can switch among these multiple sources of directional information as circumstances dictate, such as when clouds may obscure the stars. Some cues may be used to cross-check other direction indicators.

Once the migrant is underway, geomagnetism can provide a good locational map even in the absence of major geographical landmarks or celestial cues. The earth's magnetic field varies across the globe in its three-dimensional orientation and intensity; birds can sense these variations and evidently use them to navigate routes by an internal map developed during prior migrations. In essence, birds have an experience-based navigation system that is fine-tuned with each migratory journey. Because the birds know their location, experienced migrants can make course corrections if they happen to be blown off course during a storm.

As migrants approach their destination, cues from familiar local features (water bodies, landforms, or vegetation patterns, for example) kick in and allow them to find very specific sites, such as a beach, where they overwintered the previous year. For tubenose seabirds, odors emanating from nesting islands can also be important, and these sometimes operate at surprisingly long distances.

Brant pair and their seven goslings on the Alaska tundra

NOVICE MIGRANTS

Many young birds, some with only a few weeks of flying experience, complete lengthy migrations that span continents and hemispheres. Their first migratory flight, with new challenges every day, is the purest essence of an "epic journey" that we can imagine. The end of their journey—sometimes thousands of miles away, perhaps on a remote island or lake—may find them in a traditionally used wintering area, and soon they are standing or floating among experienced adults that arrived weeks earlier. These initial migrations of juveniles are forays into the unknown. How do they find their way?

Some, like young geese, have strong bonds with their parents and simply follow them along the migration route. With that experience, they acquire an internal map to use on subsequent migrations of their own. First-time migrants of many species forsake parental guidance and head off independently, often weeks after the adults have departed. These inexperienced youngsters cannot truly navigate because they have no internal map to indicate where they are. (Imagine the GPS in your car without the background map.) Instead, they use an approach that involves an instinctive response to compass information, provided by either geomagnetic or celestial cues, which tells them the direction to fly, and an internal clock that indicates when they should start and stop. If they get blown off course by strong winds, they tend to continue in their initial direction rather than chart a new route as experienced adults routinely do.

Migratory waterbirds have extraordinary navigational abilities. We know that they are keenly sensitive to many kinds of directional and locational cues, and we surmise that they continually integrate this information for increased precision as they migrate. However, the underlying mechanisms by which birds navigate flawlessly from one end of the planet to the other, year after year, remain poorly known.

The magnificent wetland corridor for waterfowl that migrate through Washington, Oregon, and California has been greatly altered by human activities. Wildlife refuges and natural wetlands now exist mostly as islands within a grid of irrigated industrial agriculture. These snow geese are flying across the Sacramento–San Joaquin Delta (California Delta), headed to nearby over-wintering areas in California's Central Valley. The determined birds remind us that given a carefully selected and appropriately managed array of favorable habitats, viable populations of migratory waterfowl can persist even in some of the most intensively human-altered landscapes.

CHAPTER 5

Migrants in a Dangerous World

The obvious and sometimes dramatic lethal effects of predation can obscure the nonlethal effects of the mere presence of predators.

—Steven Lima

DANGER ON THE WING

It's early May on the Fraser River Estuary in southwestern British Columbia. Thousands of dunlins and western sandpipers are scurrying across an expansive mudflat, feeding on a green sheen of biofilm. Suddenly, a giant cloud of shorebirds swirls skyward, tightening ranks and evasively veering left and right. The distinctive silhouette of a peregrine falcon can be seen against the sky, keeping pace with the roiling flock. The hunter targets a straggler at the edge of the flock, and drops out of the sky in the legendary dive known as a stoop. With a poof of feathers the only evidence of a successful strike, the peregrine turns back toward the shore with its prey clutched tight in its talons.

Migration is an inherently risky business, and in the hazardous realm of epic journeys, danger lurks at every turn. Severe storms, disease, and harmful algal blooms sometimes kill thousands of migrants in a day or a week. These devastating events tend to be infrequent and unpredictable, their impacts impossible to avoid. But predation danger is a near constant. The gauntlet of opportunistic predators that migrants must outwit— owls, coyotes, foxes, mink, mice, rats, feral cats and dogs, raptors, jaegers, gulls, and even snakes—poses an ever-present threat and sometimes exacts a heavy toll.

A peregrine falcon lifts off the marsh with a freshly captured whimbrel in its talons.

Peregrine falcons, formidable predators of migratory birds throughout the Pacific Americas, present a danger that waterbirds contend with year-round, but especially during the falcon migration season. They are the fastest flyers on the earth, and in horizontal pursuit of their prey, may reach speeds of 70 miles (110 km) per hour. Focusing their deadly attacks mostly on ducks and shorebirds, peregrines routinely kill up to three birds a day during the migratory season. They sometimes kill large ducks but are more attracted to smaller species, such as green-winged teals. They attack their chosen prey at any time of the year—on land, in the air, or on the water, often making several attempts before they are successful.

Each year, seasonal waves of peregrine falcons travel along the Pacific coast of North America, moving north in spring and returning south in late summer and fall. Not surprisingly, peregrine migration timing is often closely aligned with the migrations of their favorite prey. Around the Salish Sea and along the outer coast, falcon numbers peak in late April and early May as the birds move northward toward breeding sites in the northern reaches of western North America. Another wave occurs in August and September after the peregrine nesting season, as returning adults and their young head southward to their wintering areas.

A peregrine falcon flies to its cliff roost at Point Reyes National Seashore with a red phalarope in its talons.

Snowy owls are normally year-round residents of the tundra, periodically migrating south to spend the winter in tidewater wetlands and farm fields when food shortages and harsh winter conditions prevail in the far north. During these irruptive migrations large numbers of these magnificent owls appear in places like Vancouver's Boundary Bay Regional Park and in Washington's Samish, Padilla, and Skagit Bays, where they can depend on a ready supply of sea ducks, grebes, shorebirds, songbirds, and small mammals.

During a peak irruption year in the Pacific Northwest it is common to see adult and juvenile snowy owls watching for seabird or rodent prey from the tops of driftwood logs at the edge of a coastal marsh.

Long-tailed jaeger on nest

Pomarine jaeger

On the northern breeding grounds, ground-nesting waterbirds in open tundra and colonies of seabirds that nest on cliff sides may suffer major losses to predators, such as gulls and jaegers, which are very skilled at taking advantage of unguarded nests and can snatch an egg or nestling from an unwary parent in an instant. In fact, gulls are major predators of nesting waterbirds nearly everywhere. Waterbirds that nest in colonies sometimes thwart predators through group defense—effectively ganging up on would-be marauders.

Right: Predation by large-bodied gulls is a major cause of egg and chick loss for many seabird species. Terns seem to be especially vulnerable to this omnipresent threat, and are especially vigilant when they share their nesting grounds with gulls breeding nearby. Here we see a Heermann's gull at Isla Rasa, a special protected island in the Gulf of California (Mexico), being driven off by elegant terns after attempting to snatch a tern egg from a nest.

Bald eagles, best known as fish eaters, also pose a danger for migrating waterbirds along much of the Pacific coast of North America. These opportunistic predators kill or scavenge a wide range of ducks, loons, grebes, and seabirds. The frequency of bald eagle attacks on waterbirds changes with the seasons. In some areas, such as the Salish Sea, eagles are relatively scarce in late summer and early fall because most are farther north, drawn by an abundance of spawning salmon in Alaska and northern British Columbia. Once the salmon feast ends, bald eagles return to the Salish Sea and other areas along the coast of the Pacific Northwest, where their winter menu includes migratory waterbirds.

Besides being legitimate predators, bald eagles are also airborne food pirates with a taste for a free meal. They commonly chase or harass peregrine falcons that have caught a duck or dunlin, forcing them to drop their prey. Eagles also influence the falcons' choice of prey. When eagles are not actively harassing them, peregrines are more likely to attack ducks, which are larger than shorebirds and a better "to-go" food prize for the eagle.

Bald eagles often attempt to abscond with fish or birds captured by other predators. This eagle is closing in on a great blue heron that has captured a fish.

Dramatic lethal impacts of raptors can be seen along the entire length of the Pacific Americas. Less obvious is the profound influence that raptor presence has on how, when, and where waterbirds migrate. One basic antipredator tactic is to avoid foraging habitats where nearby trees or other tall vegetation provide raptors with camouflage to launch stealthy attacks. By shifting to open mudflats and other feeding sites where the camouflage cover is distant, the vigilant migrants get an early warning of a predator's imminent approach.

The dance between predator and prey—peregrine falcon and shorebird—is a survival drama that is constantly unfolding. Sandpipers, to gain the fat they need for migration, seek nutrition-rich sites. When these food larders are in places that facilitate raptor attacks, they must balance their fattening rate against their exposure to predators. Migratory sandpipers arriving at stopover sites with depleted fat reserves may opt for foraging habitats offering abundant food but less protection from predators. Migrants arriving with high fat reserves have the luxury of feeding in the relative safety of large open mudflats even if the dining buffet is skimpy.

Migrants also avoid predators by altering their routes. After nesting, many southbound western sandpipers fly nonstop over the ocean from Alaska to southern British Columbia. Falcons and other raptors are still busy raising young on their breeding grounds and are uncommon at the coastal sites in western Alaska, where the sandpipers are fattening up for their direct flight to southern British Columbia. In spring, on the northbound migration, they omit the transoceanic route and instead follow one that hugs the coast, which allows them to stop frequently and forage lightly, maintaining their advantage over predators by remaining relatively lean, fast, and maneuverable. These alterations lessen the falcon threat at this dangerous season.

The peregrine falcon predation threat has also affected the timing of sandpiper migrations. After nesting in Alaska, adult western sandpipers spend little time with their offspring. Instead, they bolt southward, starting their migration in midsummer, almost a month ahead of the peregrine migration. Their fledglings will fend for themselves for a month before heading south to wintering sites. For the adults, their nonstop transoceanic flight from coastal Alaska to southwestern British Columbia helps reduce travel time down the Pacific coast, and they arrive in Panama and other wintering areas in time to complete their monthlong molt of flight feathers before most falcons arrive.

Migratory waterbirds also change their behavior in the presence of bald eagles. Along most of coastal western North America, waterbirds are numerous during early fall migration, and many species remain common throughout the winter. The majority vacate coastal waters in early spring when they migrate to nesting areas. Bald eagles move into waterbird-rich coastal waters in increasing numbers through fall and winter, coincident with the presence of many migratory waterbirds. Diving waterbirds seem to try to avoid these airborne hunters, moving farther away from shore, where it is harder for an eagle to make a surprise attack. Dabbling ducks and scoters tend to form large flocks, making it difficult for an eagle to focus on one target. They also become more vigilant and undertake long avoidance flights. On the approach of a bald eagle, large mixed-species groups of waterbirds frequently flush en masse from the water or from roost sites; the swirling horde of alerted birds appears to discourage eagles from attempting an attack.

A Canada goose defends its young from an attack by a juvenile bald eagle.

Restoration of raptors and other predators to their former roles in the food web has led to an ongoing interplay of population and behavior adjustments as predator and prey reach a new balance. In the 1970s populations of falcons and eagles had plummeted, primarily as a result of poor reproductive success caused by ingestion of pesticide-contaminated food and exacerbated by a long history of mortality from wanton shooting. With the ban of DDT use in North America, better protection, and the initiation of reintroduction programs, raptor populations have rebounded, and these birds have resumed their ecological roles in the lives of migratory waterbirds.

Prior to the 1990s, dunlins roosted in exposed sites on the Fraser River Estuary when their foraging beaches were inundated at high tide. As the falcon population recovered from the impacts of DDT, dunlins began to form massive swirling flocks over the bay for up to several hours during high tide. The spectacularly synchronized but unpredictable gyrations of a dense fast-flying flock appear to inhibit falcon attacks by making it difficult for a falcon to isolate a target or make a strike without risking injury from a collision. This prolonged aerial flocking behavior, which does not occur at night when the falcons are inactive, exacts a high energetic cost that dunlins can afford because of the high productivity of the Fraser River Estuary.

Avian predators in the Pacific Americas play an influential role in shaping the migrations of waterbirds. Migrating shorebirds, ducks, and other waterbirds balance danger from predators against their nesting and nutritional requirements as they make complicated choices about when and where to migrate and molt, how much fat to carry, and how much time to spend feeding and breeding. It's a vital natural process.

A bald eagle harasses a northwestern crow.

CHAPTER 6

Migration Marathoners

Now they pass, filling the distance,
a faint flapping of wings against the light,
a throbbing winged unity . . .

—Pablo Neruda, Art of Birds

Western sandpipers and dunlins rest along the mudflats of Alaska's Copper River Delta during spring migration.

It's late April on the vast tidal mudflats of Alaska's Copper River Delta, one of the most important migratory staging areas of the Pacific Americas. The arrivals and northbound departures of countless waterbird flocks create a shimmering haze against the dramatic backdrop of snowcapped mountains. As many as 5 million shorebirds will rest and feed here during spring migration. For most of these migrants this will be the final refueling stopover on their long journey to the Arctic breeding grounds.

Along the distant horizon, where the wilderness estuary system meets the sea, a lens-shaped cloud twists and turns as it moves toward shore. Sometimes the cloud vanishes over the dark water only to reappear like a burst of confetti against the blue sky. The cloud crystallizes into a giant shape-shifting flock of western sandpipers and dunlins—thousands of birds moving as one.

The swirling flock passes overhead and abruptly reverses direction, flashing light-colored breasts and darker backs as the birds bank and roll with palpable energy.

A crescendo of spirited voices and a feather-softened whir of thousands of beating wings accompany the passing aerial choreography. Slowing as they approach shore, the sandpipers descend with exaggerated wingbeats and land on the mudflat, aligning nearly side by side. Facing the wind, they pull up one foot and tuck their bills backward in repose. Some of these little migrants have traveled more than 5,000 miles (8,000 km) since last month.

Birders and nature enthusiasts from around the world migrate to the annual Copper River Delta Shorebird Festival in Cordova, Alaska, to experience this incredible migratory phenomenon.

Inset: The food-rich mudflats of Alaska's Copper River Delta sustain millions of migrating sandpipers—the largest concentrated passage of shorebirds in the Western Hemisphere.

Dunlin

Semipalmated plovers

Black oystercatcher

Black-necked stilts

CAST OF CHARACTERS

The word *shorebird* refers collectively to species from four distinctive families of waterbirds: sandpipers, plovers, oystercatchers, and the avocets and stilts. Differences in body size and proportions, bill shape, plumage coloration, and behavior reveal their rich ecological diversification. The smallest North American shorebird is the aptly named least sandpiper. At the other end of the scale are long-billed curlews and oystercatchers. The color variations in shorebird plumages, whether it be the bold disruptive coloration of semipalmated plovers— the long red legs and black-and-white elegance of black-necked stilts, or the jet-black body, red bill, and pink legs of black oystercatchers—serve impressively in both attraction displays and camouflage.

83

A DAZZLING DIVERSITY OF MIGRATION PATTERNS

Shorebirds are the earth's quintessential globe-trotters, undertaking spectacular long-distance migrations between their breeding grounds and their overwintering refugia. Most shorebirds spend the majority of the year in nonbreeding areas and migrating, with just a scant few months in their breeding grounds. Arctic nesting marathoners, such as bar-tailed godwits, Hudsonian godwits, bristle-thighed curlews, and Pacific golden plovers, routinely make spectacular multiday flights of several thousand miles—nonstop! Several Arctic-nesting shorebird species travel more than 15,000 miles (24,000 km) to complete their annual circuits, making stops to rest and refuel in a dozen or more countries.

The Arctic regions of North America and northeastern Asia play a key role in the life cycle of many shorebird species. At least thirty-two species nest north of the Arctic Circle in Russia, Alaska, or northwestern Canada. By nesting in the land of the midnight sun, they are able to take advantage of long days and bountiful food while raising young. Despite strong ties to the Arctic, many Pacific Americas shorebirds are very much at home in the Southern Hemisphere, taking advantage of long summer days in both hemispheres. More than two dozen shorebird species make long-distance migrations from North America to nonbreeding habitats as far away as Central and South America. Nearly a million shorebirds spend the winter in Mexico and California, and even more continue south along the wild edge of the Pacific. More than a million migrating sandpipers visit beaches in Panama, and hundreds of thousands stay through the winter.

Ruddy turnstones nest on coastal tundra in the Arctic, but winter along wave-swept rocky or sandy shorelines in more southerly latitudes.

Shorebirds are determined nesters. A late spring snowfall in Alaska did not stop this killdeer from raising a brood!

In mid-April, most of these dunlins (in flight) are still wearing their winter feathers, while the black-bellied plovers below them have nearly completed their molt into breeding plumage.

85

Several shorebird populations that breed in the Arctic regions of North America completely abandon the Pacific Flyway in winter and end up in eastern Asia. Others travel far to the east of the Pacific Americas for major portions of their journeys, sometimes making large one-way loops. Whimbrels nesting on the Mackenzie River Delta in the far northeastern Pacific Flyway migrate eastward across North America and over the open Atlantic Ocean to wintering sites in coastal Brazil. Some sanderling populations migrate along the Pacific Flyway going both north and south, while others trace a huge loop that involves a southbound flight along the Pacific coast and northbound migration through central North America or along the Atlantic coast.

The word *shorebird* suggests that this group of waterbirds tends to stay along coastal areas as they migrate between their nesting and wintering grounds. While this generalization is true for some shorebird species, many others take seasonal advantage of habitats well inland from the coast, including freshwater and saline wetlands, lakes and ponds, rivers, open grasslands, and deserts.

Some species, such as black turnstones, black oystercatchers, surfbirds, ruddy turnstones, and rock sandpipers, largely restrict their lives to the narrow margin of the Pacific Flyway's coastal shores. After nesting in western Alaska, black turnstones migrate south along the coast and many spend the winter along rocky shores as far south as Baja California and the Gulf of California. Their narrow migration route rarely deviates from the coast, and turnstones rarely leave the Pacific Americas.

Hudsonian godwits that nest in south-central Alaska fly a consistent—and stunning—migration route each year. Individual godwits make weeklong nonstop flights of more than 6,200 miles (9,980 km) going north and five-day flights exceeding 4,000 miles (6,430 km) going south. Hudsonian godwits are among the many shorebirds that link the resources of different flyways into unique migratory lifeways.

Ruddy turnstones (breeding plumage)

Rock sandpiper

Black oystercatchers are basically homebodies that stay near their breeding grounds year-round, but a few explorers have been spotted a thousand miles from where they hatched. Some surfbirds and ruddy turnstones migrate between Alaska and the far southern reaches of the Pacific Americas in southern South America, but many individuals of both species never venture beyond Mexico. The surfbird's winter/nonbreeding range is the longest and narrowest of any waterbird in the Pacific Flyway.

Thousands of rock sandpipers spend the winter in Alaska's upper Cook Inlet, the world's coldest and most northerly location known to support overwintering populations of shorebirds. Such conditions come at a high energetic cost, one that demands energy-rich food and an accelerated rate of foraging to keep the metabolic fires burning. Rock sandpipers meet this demand by eating tremendous numbers of tiny macoma clams. Shore-fast ice sometimes limits access to clams, so the birds focus on sites where ice-inhibiting currents and tides expose the bivalve banquet table, and they watch for new foraging opportunities exposed by the scouring action of moving icebergs.

Shorebird migrations can vary enormously even within a single species. Some populations and individuals complete supersized migrations that stretch between the far northern and southern reaches of the Pacific Americas, while other members of these same species are short-distance migrants that never leave North America. Adults and juveniles or males and females sometimes use separate migration pathways and may even fly to different wintering areas, and they may embark on their journeys at different times. Juveniles often remain in their first overwintering area for a year or more, until they are ready to breed.

Ruddy turnstones

You must look carefully at this black oystercatcher nest to identify the eggs.

Most red knots that nest in northwestern Alaska spend the winter in Baja California, but some migrate an additional 5,500 miles (8,800 km) to wintering sites in southern Chile.

Facing page: Camouflage perfected—a western sandpiper nest and eggs on the Alaska tundra.

Red foxes are significant predators on ground-nesting birds throughout much of North America. Non-native populations have been particularly destructive to migratory and resident waterbirds.

ON THE NESTING GROUNDS

Most North American shorebirds, and nearly all sandpipers, breed in northern latitudes, where a seasonal abundance of food fuels the reproductive activities of millions of adult shorebirds and the rapid growth of their young. When shorebirds arrive on their Arctic breeding grounds, they settle in quickly, bursting into song with an urgent vibrancy focused on attracting a mate and staking out a nesting territory. Their full-voiced chorale is often a mixture of the beautiful and the haunting, accompanied by elaborate flight displays. Shorebirds are nest-design minimalists, and most nests are little more than a shallow scrape softened with grasses and bits of lichen. Nesting sites are typically on elevated patches of tundra that provide a clear view of approaching airborne predators, such as peregrines and jaegers,

or opportunistic predators such as foxes. Feathery camouflage and stalwart vigilance are crucial to survival and breeding success.

By early to mid-August, the fleeting arctic summer gives way to shorter days, cooler temperatures, and the first hints of autumn color in the tundra. Many adult shorebirds have already departed on their southbound journeys, leaving behind juveniles that have just grown their first set of flight feathers. Many juvenile shorebirds, such as young black-bellied plovers, remain in southern nonbreeding areas for their first year and migrate north to the breeding grounds when they are almost two years old. For these nonbreeders, one advantage of staying south may be a lower risk of predation by peregrine falcons and merlins, many of which spend the spring and summer to the north of the juvenile plovers.

Black-necked stilts that nest in North America are short- to medium-distance migrants. This female and chick are on the breeding grounds of San Francisco Bay, California, where many stilts also spend the winter.

American avocets and black-necked stilts in the Pacific Flyway often share the same breeding and nonbreeding habitats, such as this wintering area in the Gulf of California, Mexico. Studies in the Great Basin of North America suggest that the young may sometimes migrate with their siblings when they depart from natal ponds and wetlands.

The spring and fall migration seasons often afford the best opportunities for watching shorebirds and observing their unique foraging behaviors. A visit to the outer Pacific coast of North America often yields views of a dozen or more species—sanderlings, marbled godwits, willets, and semipalmated plovers on sandy beaches; western sandpipers, dunlins, dowitchers, and black-bellied plovers on mudflats; avocets and stilts in muddy ponds; and black turnstones and surfbirds on rocky shores. The shorebird diet includes a diversity of invertebrate delicacies, such as marine worms, tiny crustaceans (shrimp, crabs, barnacles, and sand fleas), and small mollusks (snails, limpets, clams, and mussels), and insects and their larvae.

A pair of marbled godwits pass a marine worm back and forth in what may be courtship behavior prior to mating. Marbled godwits nest in meadows near lakes and ponds in the northern Great Plains but stay only long enough to raise their young. They spend the next eight to nine months taking advantage of the abundant food resources on Pacific beaches and mudflats along the North American coast.

Long-billed dowitchers are tactile foragers and use their sturdy bills, the tip of which is covered with tiny sensors, to probe mud or wet sand in a distinctive sewing machine–like manner in their search for invertebrate prey.

The tremendous diversity in the lengths and shapes of shorebird bills—long, short, upturned, downturned, wedge-like, straight, or slightly curved—and how the bird uses it are unique to each species. Some use their bills for probing, picking at the surface, or as wedges to open hard-shelled prey. Leg length also plays a key role in determining each shorebird's distinct foraging niche. Long-billed shorebirds are able to probe deeper in wet sand or mud than short-billed species, and long-legged shorebirds are able to wade and forage in deeper water than short-legged species.

A shorebird's bill may look rigid, much like a pair of chopsticks, but the upper jaw of many species can bend and flex open near the bill tip while the rest of the jaw remains closed or slightly open. Such rhynchokinesis, which can be seen in the bill of this long-billed curlew, appears to increase the efficiency of capturing and feeding on small food items buried in the mud or suspended in water. Most shorebird species have bills in which the tip and surface of the bill are equipped with thousands of tiny pits that contain specialized sensory organs, allowing them to detect hidden food items and distinguish them as edible by touch, and some species can even sense—through pressure gradients—the presence of tiny clams just beyond the reach of their probing bills.

Oystercatchers are named for their dietary preference for shellfish and for their prowess in opening hard-shelled prey such as mussels, clams, and other mollusks. A quick jab with their blade-shaped bill cuts the adductor muscle and makes quick work of most bivalves. They use their bills to forage on crabs and urchins and in a chisel-like manner to remove limpets and chitons from rocky surfaces. They also probe for marine worms and other soft-bodied prey.

Long-billed curlew

American avocets usually wade while feeding, sweeping their upcurved bills through water or silt in search of tiny prey. The bill is pointed at the tip for probing and picking, and the inner margins of the bill have minute structures that function like a filter in capturing food particles while they bill-sweep. Avocets have webbed feet and are good swimmers, sometimes paddling into deeper water and dabbling, head down, like ducks. On the wintering grounds, avocets will often gather in large groups and forage cooperatively, with individual birds all taking advantage of or prey items (small fish or tiny crustaceans) disturbed by others, which increases each bird's chance of success.

These overwintering American avocets are foraging as a group in the alkaline waters along Mexico's Colorado River Delta. Sometimes walking forward in unison, the avocets swing their upcurved bills back and forth through the water to capture tiny invertebrates.

Phalaropes have paddle-like toes with small flaps that facilitate swimming on the water surface as the birds feed on small invertebrates. By swimming rapidly in tight circles, phalaropes create currents that bring submerged food closer to the surface.

The long legs of black-necked stilts, American avocets, and greater yellowlegs allow them to wade and forage in deeper waters than other shorebirds.

A flock of marbled godwits settles down to roost.

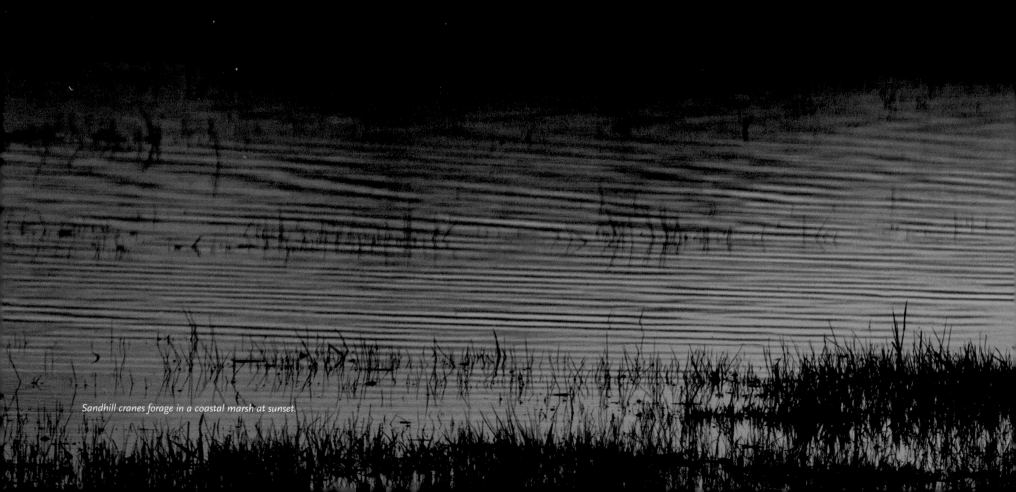

CHAPTER 7

The Voices of Migration

Sandhill cranes forage in a coastal marsh at sunset.

These voices . . . carry through misty winds and above the white
sound of driven waters. . . . They are tuned by the landscape—
they are voices of the land. . . . To my ear all these voices,
in their innocent melancholy and exuberance,
reach to that place where laughter and tears meld,
and life celebrates itself upon the land.

—Jeff Fair, *Arctic Wings*

On Russia's Wrangel Island the cold wind that sweeps off the Chukchi Sea is relentless, ice crystals sparkling in the sunshine. Despite patches of lingering snow, there are hints of green and the scent of the coastal tundra coming to life. In the distance, the voices of hundreds of snow geese blend in an excited cacophony as they come flying in from across the sea to their Arctic home. The vibrant voices of geese mark the changing seasons with an unquenchable exuberance—the timeless music of an enduring rite of passage.

The smallest waterfowl in the northern Pacific Americas—buffleheads, ruddy ducks, and teal—are dedicated migrants. Although weighing only slightly more than a trumpeter swan egg, these little ducks easily make migrations exceeding 1,000 miles (1,600 km).

GEESE, SWANS, AND DUCKS

Blue-winged teal, although small in stature, migrate farther south than any other North American duck. On the breeding grounds, Pacific Flyway teal nest and molt quickly, heading off to overwintering wetlands in northern California and as far south as Central and South America.

Twice a year, millions of migrating waterfowl—geese, swans, and ducks—finesse the winds aloft and undertake journeys charted and fine-tuned by their ancestors over the millennia. The Pacific Flyway offers an extraordinary diversity of inland wetlands and coastal waters that attract and sustain tremendous legions of migratory waterfowl. An estimated 5 million waterfowl winter in the Central Valley of California, but this is perhaps only one-tenth of the historical total. These waterfowl come from nesting areas extending from the Arctic tundra of northeastern Asia and Alaska as well as from the prairies of interior North America and local breeding sites in the Central Valley. Pacific coastal estuaries harbor an abundance of wintering waterfowl, particularly brant and diving ducks. Many of the scoters, goldeneyes, long-tailed ducks, harlequin ducks, and mergansers you see along the coast may have come from breeding ponds and wetlands deep within the interior of western North America.

Of the forty-two waterfowl species that nest in North America, most of the southbound flow of migrants will overwinter somewhere between southeast Alaska and California, with a few continuing south to Mexico. A few species—notably emperor geese and spectacled eiders—rarely stray from the tundra regions of the far north. In contrast, blue-winged teal—widespread nesters in Canada and the continental United States—are champions among duck migrants, with a winter range that extends from the southern states through much of South America. No matter the distance or destination, waterfowl remind us of the uniqueness of each migratory journey and the sometimes-surprising places waterbirds call home.

Tundra swans on their nesting habitat in the National Petroleum Reserve in northern Alaska.

Emperor geese, short-distance migrants, rarely leave the Bering Sea region. In western Alaska, home to the largest populations, emperors nest on coastal tundra and most winter close to the rocky intertidal zone in the Aleutian Islands, the southern coast of the Alaska Peninsula, and on Afognak and Kodiak Islands.

Trumpeter swans, named for their deep bugle-like calls, nest in scattered areas along the Pacific Flyway, northward to central Alaska, with the highest concentrations on the Yukon-Kuskokwim Delta, and in western Canada. During autumn, small flocks of trumpeters migrate as necessary to find sheltered open water sites as far south as California. The thrill of seeing them is the fruit of a conservation success story, as populations have rebounded from historical overharvesting.

Waterfowl migrations, even those confined to North America, sometimes show striking variations in the routes chosen by different populations of the same species. Tundra swans that nest in western Alaska migrate through the interior of western North America or along the Pacific coast as they shift to their winter quarters in central California. In striking contrast, most swans that nest in northern Alaska and the nearby Mackenzie River Delta migrate 3,400 miles (5,500 km) southeastward across North America to spend the winter on the US mid-Atlantic coast, a continent away from their western Alaska brethren.

SMALL GEESE, BOLD TRAVELERS

Peter Steinhart, in his book *Tracks in the Sky*, described the Pacific Flyway as "a reflection of the water below the sky." In the vast and watery realm of the Alaska Arctic, these words capture the vital essence of Izembek Lagoon National Wildlife Refuge. Izembek's location near the southwestern tip of the Alaska Peninsula, near the beginning of the 1,000-mile (1,609-km) arc of the Aleutian Islands, makes it a global migratory crossroads for hundreds of thousands of Arctic-breeding waterbirds.

The allure for waterfowl is abundant food—a feast provided by the lagoon's luxuriant swards of eelgrass and the diversity of invertebrates and fish eggs and larvae that thrive in these marine ecosystems. Izembek Lagoon contains the world's largest expanses of eelgrass. This food resource supports more than 90 percent of the Pacific population of brant as well as the world's population of spectacled and Steller's eider and large numbers of tundra swans.

Mount Dutton and Isanotski Volcano provide a dramatic backdrop for Izembek Lagoon National Wildlife Refuge—a migratory hot spot for waterfowl and shorebirds dominated by shallow marine lagoons and freshwater wetlands. For brant, seen here, the refuge serves as a key staging area during spring and fall migrations.

The highly migratory Pacific population of brant nests in the coastal Arctic region of Russia, Alaska, and northwestern Canada. A brant tagged in a nesting area in north-central Russia was seen in winter in Morro Bay, California, after a migratory journey of about 4,800 miles (7,725 km). This Alaska tundra-nesting brant is sitting at the edge of her downy nest with two recently hatched chicks. Brant eggs mostly hatch simultaneously, but sometimes hatching continues over the span of a couple days. It appears that the central egg is just hatching.

After nesting, Arctic geese move to regions where they undergo molt prior to migration. They seek remote waters with minimal human disturbance, low predation risk, and an abundance of the nutrient-rich foods needed for growing new feathers. Tens of thousands of brant, cackling geese, greater white-fronted geese, and snow geese fly to the Teshekpuk Lake area of the National Petroleum Reserve in northern Alaska to complete this molt, which renders them flightless and vulnerable.

Like certain shorebirds, some migrating waterfowl aim seaward and boldly set out on long flights over the open ocean, forsaking the feeding and resting stops available along the coast. When southbound from Alaska, brant fatten up over several weeks while feeding on eelgrass in Izembek Lagoon on the Alaska Peninsula and then fly southeastward across the ocean to their wintering areas, primarily on bays, lagoons, and estuaries in Baja California (Mexico). The brant exodus from the lagoon sometimes involves a spectacular departure of more than 100,000 birds on a single day! The transoceanic route to Baja California entails a daunting nonstop flight of 3,300 miles (5,300 km) over two to four days (tough winds and bad weather may slow the flight). It's a direct but energetically costly trip. By the time the determined migrants arrive in Baja, they've burned up their stored fat and lost up to one-third of their initial body weight.

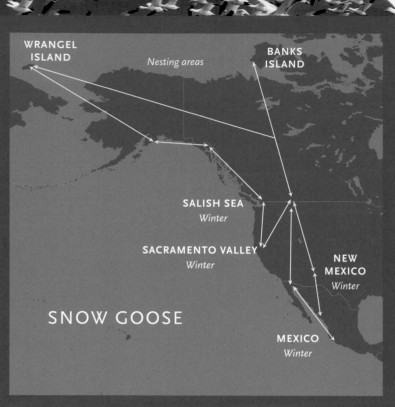

SNOW GOOSE

WRANGEL
ISLAND

Nesting areas

BANKS
ISLAND

SALISH SEA
Winter

SACRAMENTO VALLEY
Winter

NEW
MEXICO
Winter

MEXICO
Winter

Snow goose migrations entail some intriguing route variations and long-distance con-nections between specific nesting and wintering areas. Populations that nest on Wrangel Island, in northern Alaska, and in the western Canadian Arctic (primarily Banks Island), winter on the Salish Sea coast or in areas farther south, primarily California's Central Valley. Snow geese migrating southward from Wrangel Island follow a primarily coastal route, but some individuals include a long nonstop flight over the ocean between Alaska and British Columbia, and others take a circuitous inland route that passes through the prairie wetlands of southern Alberta and Saskatchewan. Knowledge of these unique and unpredictable migration patterns is critical to developing protection and management plans that safeguard populations through their full annual cycle.

A BLIZZARD OUT OF THE ARCTIC

Snow geese are among the most abundant and "watchable" of western North America's migratory waterfowl. The two largest breeding populations (Wrangel Island and Banks Island) each host hundreds of thousands of nesting geese, and populations in northern Alaska have skyrocketed. Immense overwintering flocks are a common sight on wildlife refuges and in agricultural fields around the Salish Sea and southward through California to Mexico, wherever marshes and fields provide abundant and predictable food resources. Visitors to the most important wintering areas, such as the Skagit River Estuary in Washington, Fraser River Delta in British Columbia, and California's Sacramento Valley, often experience the sight and sound extravaganza of thousands of snow geese sweeping overhead in an electrifying white blizzard.

DUCK TALES

Dabbling ducks, such as mallards, northern pintails, northern shovelers, and several species of teal, forage by skimming the water surface with their bills or by upending to reach submerged vegetation or small prey. Dabblers have short legs and webbed feet positioned midway up the body, which makes moving on land easier and, when combined with lower wing–loading, allows them to spring directly into the air on takeoff rather than pattering across the water surface. The migrations and midwinter movements of dabbling ducks are focused mostly on ice-free freshwater sites or sheltered coastal waters.

Most dabblers, such as this northern shoveler, have small comblike structures (lamellae), along the inside edges of their bills that function like a sieve in straining food items from water or soupy mud.

Northern pintails wintering in California's Central Valley reach nesting areas in western Alaska by three main routes: one along the Pacific coast, another over the open ocean, and the other via a looping detour through Canada's prairie wetlands. These diverse migration paths likely developed in conjunction with environmental changes since the Last Glacial Maximum about 18,000 years ago, when ice sheets and large lakes covered much of the pintails' current breeding range and migration paths.

Mallard family

Bufflehead chick

Diving ducks are well adapted to a life spent on the water. They have large paddle-like feet, legs situated far back on the body, and short tails—an awkward design on land, but one that provides superb propulsion when diving. Divers stroke with their strong webbed feet to reach the bottom to obtain their favorite foods, which range from plant material (canvasbacks) to clams and mussels (scoters and eiders) and fish (mergansers). Most diving ducks, such as buffleheads, ruddy ducks, goldeneyes, and mergansers, spend the winter in coastal waters, but some take advantage of ice-free inland ponds, lakes, and rivers. Sea ducks, such as scoters and eiders, spend time on land only to breed; during the nonbreeding season, they inhabit remote coastal habitats and the open ocean. To escape danger, diving ducks have the edge on dabblers and can swim great distances underwater to elude aerial predators.

Mallard drake

Most waterfowl nest on the ground, but a few diving ducks (bufflehead, common goldeneye, and common merganser) nest in tree cavities. This nesting strategy requires the ducklings, like this bufflehead, to leap to the ground and follow their mother to water just hours after they hatch.

Bufflehead (adult male)

Not all waterfowl migrate to the beat of the same drum—flight schedules vary according to the ecological requirements of each species and the geographic location and environmental conditions where they breed. Along the Pacific Northwest coast, southbound American wigeons and green-winged teal arrive in numbers in September before summer's warmth ends, whereas large influxes of common goldeneyes and buffleheads do not appear until freezing weather arrives in November and December. Males and failed breeders commonly migrate earlier than birds absorbed with parental duties.

Male harlequin ducks are seen along their inland breeding streams and rivers in spring and early summer. They depart for coastal waters in June or early July. Females with broods may not migrate until August, September, or October.

During migration thousands of surf scoters gather in immense flocks—a black feathered blanket spangled with the gleaming white head patches of the males. When a flock is about to move, the volume of their chortling voices rises, and soon the whole assembly sprints over the water, churning the surface with running feet and beating wings. As the scoters take off, the air resounds with a loud throbbing whistle as thousands of wings cut the air—another of the magnificent sounds of migration.

ELEGANT SOJOURNERS

In "Marshland Elegy" Aldo Leopold described the voice of the sandhill crane as "the trumpet in the orchestra of evolution." His eloquent words speak not only to the antiquity of cranes but also to the cranes' remarkable vocalizations. Sandhill cranes have an exceptionally long trachea (windpipe), which coils complexly against the breastbone, functioning much like an avian version of a brass horn.

In June 1924, ornithologist Herbert Brandt explored the wetland wilderness of the Yukon-Kuskokwim Delta in a sealskin kayak with two Yup'ik boys as guides. Brandt was a member of the first expedition to study Arctic breeding birds along the Bering Sea coastline of western Alaska. While helping him search for the nests and eggs of the "little brown crane" (sandhill crane), the boys spotted a pair at a nest along the shoreline. One boy took his blunt-tipped bird arrow and used it to drum on the kayak's deck as both began a singsong chant. In the midst of their defensive territorial display, the crane pair began to move in a dancelike manner, arching their necks and pausing after each set of movements. When the boys drummed and sang faster, the "dancers" did the same. Brandt described this amazing experience as "the only occasion on which a bird couple danced an ornithologist out of a very acceptable set of eggs."

Along the Pacific Flyway sandhill cranes nest in Arctic tundra, in muskeg bogs, on small mossy islets in beaver ponds, and in meadows along tidal creeks. Mated pairs often spontaneously call in unison, with their bills pointed skyward. Adult sandhill cranes often become stained a rusty or cinnamon color when they preen iron-rich mud onto their otherwise plain-gray feathers. The reddish stain—or "cosmetic coloration"—is thought to provide camouflage while nesting, but it might also function in behavioral interactions. Rusty feather margins in juveniles are part of the plumage pigmentation rather than staining.

Sandhill cranes nesting in south-central Alaska typically winter in the Central Valley of California.

The migration covers approximately 2,400 miles (3,860 km), includes many stops, and takes about one month southbound but twice as long going north. The Central Valley wetlands and fields needed by sandhill cranes for roosting and foraging have been diminished by expanding vineyards, orchards, and urbanization. The nesting sandhill cranes admired by Brandt were part of a large population that migrates along an interior North American route to wintering habitats in Texas, New Mexico, Arizona, and northern Mexico. This interior route is shared with cranes that nest much farther north, across a wide region extending from northeastern Russia to northwestern Canada.

Adult cranes preen their feathers with rust-colored mud to provide protective camouflage during the nesting season. Note that the chick's feathers have a natural rusty coloring at birth, which disappears as they mature.

Note that the elaborate displays of sandhill cranes are often called mating, or courtship, dances, but these intriguing behaviors may occur in any season, and some of them signify conflict or aggression. In the context of courtship and mating, the displays include a series of leaps, hops, skips, and turns, accompanied by interactive and mutual calling. Courting birds often run with their wings outstretched and toss sticks or tufts of grass into the air.

Sandhill cranes

CHAPTER 8

The Diving Life

Even the shores seemed hushed and waiting for the first lone call,
and when it came, a single long-drawn mournful note,
the quiet was deeper than before.

—Sigurd Olson, author and naturalist

There is something about the ethereal, haunting call of a common loon in the boreal twilight that makes you stop, lift your kayak paddle out of the water, and simply listen. The language of loons—the wails, tremolos, and yodels—strikes a primeval chord that resonates across time. The voices of loons embody the essence of wilderness, a compelling reminder of our role as stewards in preserving the complex, delicately balanced ecosystems that millions of animals depend on for their survival.

Although we see a few nonbreeding loons in summer along the Pacific coast, we eagerly await the onset of autumn migration, when the vast majority of loons, together with a big influx of grebes, make the seasonal shift to the saltwater habitats where they will overwinter. Most loons and grebes have spent the summer nesting and rearing young on lakes, ponds, and wetlands on coastal tundra or in the interior northern parts of the continent. Their convergence along the Pacific coast during the nonbreeding season is driven by their need for ice-free waters and a predictable and abundant source of small fishes and other foods.

Pacific Flyway red-throated loons breed in the Arctic and subarctic coastal regions of western North America and northeastern Russia. Like other loon species, they are very vocal in pair-bonding and territorial behaviors. Researchers refer to one of their strangest vocalizations, a loud and unnerving rolling growl, as the "Plesiosaur call." This call, in sharp contrast to the hauntingly beautiful cries of other loons, is often delivered as part of a pair duet and a water-based racing display.

Common loon calling

Young loons and grebes, such as these common loon and western grebe chicks, frequently ride on the backs of their parents, where they can shelter between the adults' wings and keep warm.

Loons and grebes are not closely related in an evolutionary sense, but they share several important traits and a lifestyle thoroughly devoted to the water, spending nearly all their time floating and diving. They have large feet and legs set far back on the body—ideal for diving and swimming but awkward for walking on land. Loons have three webbed front toes, and grebes have lobed paddle-like toes. Diving is foot-propelled, and their small wings are held tight to the body and used only to assist with quick underwater maneuvers. When swimming, loons do not suspend their legs under the body but extend them laterally, using them like oars for maximum thrust.

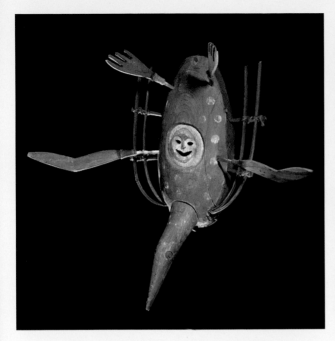

Yup'ik diving loon spirit mask with central carved human face design (circa 1870s).

After a bout of feather preening, loons often rise partway out of the water and give a vigorous shake.

This western grebe is raising its leg and lobed toes in a behavior called "foot-waggling." This behavior is most often associated with preening and resting, but thermoregulation may also play a role.

A Pacific loon emerges from a dive with beads of water glittering on its feathered head. (Arctic National Wildlife Refuge)

Prior to diving, loons and grebes compress their dense waterproof plumage, which makes them less buoyant and creates a streamlined dry suit that enables them to stay submerged while pursuing prey. After repeated dives, loons and grebes carefully preen their feathers, a process that ends with a flurry of wing flapping that helps them shed excess water and realign flight feathers.

Loons and grebes are heavy for their wing size, and most species require a long running takeoff across the water surface to get airborne. Although they must work hard in flight to stay aloft, they are strong fliers and highly migratory, setting off seasonally on long-distance flights over land and water.

These western grebe parents may be feeding their newly hatched chick its first feathers. Feather-eating behavior in grebes, which occurs from birth throughout adulthood, is unique among birds. The behavior plays a critical role in helping grebes digest and process the small fish and other animal prey in their diet. Once ingested, the feathers form a small ball (called a bolus) in the bird's gizzard that retains food long enough to allow for digestion and a second "feather filter" that keeps small bones and indigestible food items from entering the intestine. Periodically, the feathers and indigestible bits are regurgitated in the form of a pellet.

Eared grebe chicks spend their first week warm and dry atop their parents' back. Back-brooding ends when the chicks are about two weeks old. By three weeks, all parental care ceases and the adults often depart the breeding area before the young can fly. Here, an adult offers a hearty meal of dragonfly larva to the chicks.

Red-necked grebes

Western grebes

Western grebes

The display choreography of loons and grebes ranges from elaborate and highly ritualized courtship behaviors to those that seem more spontaneous and focused on territorial issues. One display behavior by red-necked grebes (top left) consists of the pair alternately floating and dipping their heads in unison. Upending and diving simultaneously, they reappear at the surface and face each other, assuming the erect and open-winged posture typically associated with courtship or pair-bonding. Western grebe displays (center, top right, and bottom) can be noisy affairs or elegantly dramatic, such as the boisterous "races" across the water or the formalized "weed rush" where the grebes foot-paddle towards each other and then assume an erect posture with nesting material in their bills.

Eared grebes are the most abundant grebe species in the world and the most social. They nest on ramshackle mounded platforms of matted reeds in shallow wetlands in the semiarid interior of western Canada and the United States. During the peak of the breeding season, their colonies resemble the grebe version of a busy marina, sometimes with hundreds of pairs nesting almost side by side.

After nesting, grebes commonly embark on "molt migrations" that take them to good feeding areas where they can undergo a simultaneous molt of their flight feathers, which renders them temporarily flightless. Red-necked grebes and western grebes fly to specific coastal waters to complete this molt and then continue southward to wintering areas. Western grebes that nest on large lakes that remain ice-free in winter may stay put and molt on the same waters used for breeding. Horned grebes tend to move to large inland lakes to molt before proceeding to their coastal wintering areas. Similarly, in late winter thousands of Pacific loons concentrate along the west coast of Baja California as they complete their flightless molt period prior to migrating northward to their nesting grounds.

Eared grebes provide a fascinating example of the complex interplay between molt, flightlessness, and migration. After nesting on lakes and ponds in interior western North America, nearly the entire population of these little red-eyed divers assembles for up to several months on hypersaline (extremely salty) lakes in the Great Basin, primarily Great Salt Lake (Utah) and Mono Lake (California). About 1.5 million individuals—about half the North American population—assemble on Great Salt Lake. While on these lakes the grebes' digestive organs grow and their flight muscles shrink to the point of flightlessness, which commonly lasts for three to four months. As the grebes gorge on brine flies and brine shrimp, their enhanced food-processing system allows them to accumulate fuel reserves in the form of thick layers of fat and grow a whole new set of wing and body feathers.

A few weeks prior to the eared grebes' departure from the lakes in fall or early winter, their physiological processes shift from growing new feathers and building fuel reserves to maximizing flight capacity. Mobilizing their fat stores, they increase the size of their flight and heart muscles. Simultaneously they jettison excess weight by shrinking the size of digestive organs. Toned and "tuned up," the grebes fly nonstop to the Salton Sea or the main wintering area in the Gulf of California. This final leg of the journey can be hazardous; thousands of grebes departing Great Salt Lake sometimes get caught in snowstorms and experience heavy mortality when they are forced to the ground.

The profound organ-size changes that accompany the migratory lifestyle of eared grebes are the most dramatic known for any bird. They occur multiple times each year, during each pause in the migration cycle, precluding flight for up to nine to ten months each year (molt of the flight feathers occurs only once each year and takes about thirty-five to forty days). Except for penguins and a handful of other birds that cannot fly, no other bird species is as aquatic and flightless for such long periods.

UNEXPECTED LOON MIGRATION ROUTES

Loons display some puzzling migration patterns. Some common loons that nest on lakes in Saskatchewan migrate southwestward to winter along the Pacific Flyway on the coast of Baja California, but others head off to wintering waters on the Louisiana coast—and some arrive there by way of a wide detour to the mid-Atlantic coast. Pacific loons also diverge widely in their migration routes and destinations. Those nesting in southwestern Alaska winter along the North American Pacific coast. In spring vast numbers of these loons can be seen migrating northward back to Alaska. During the peak migration, up to a few thousand loons pass by coastal headlands each hour. Pacific loons that nest in northern Alaska just west of the Mackenzie River Delta do something entirely different—after breeding they head west and south to spend the winter in eastern Asia. These surprising route variations are but two of many such enigmatic migration patterns that have been revealed in recent years through modern tracking technology.

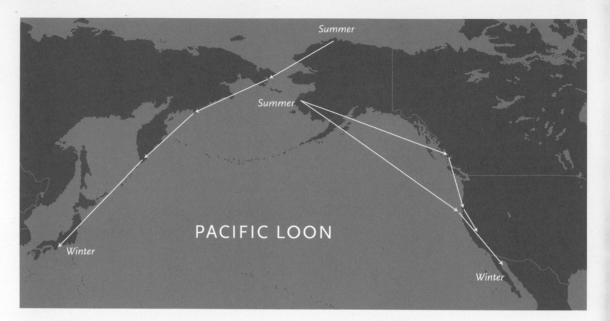

Summer

Summer

PACIFIC LOON

Winter

Winter

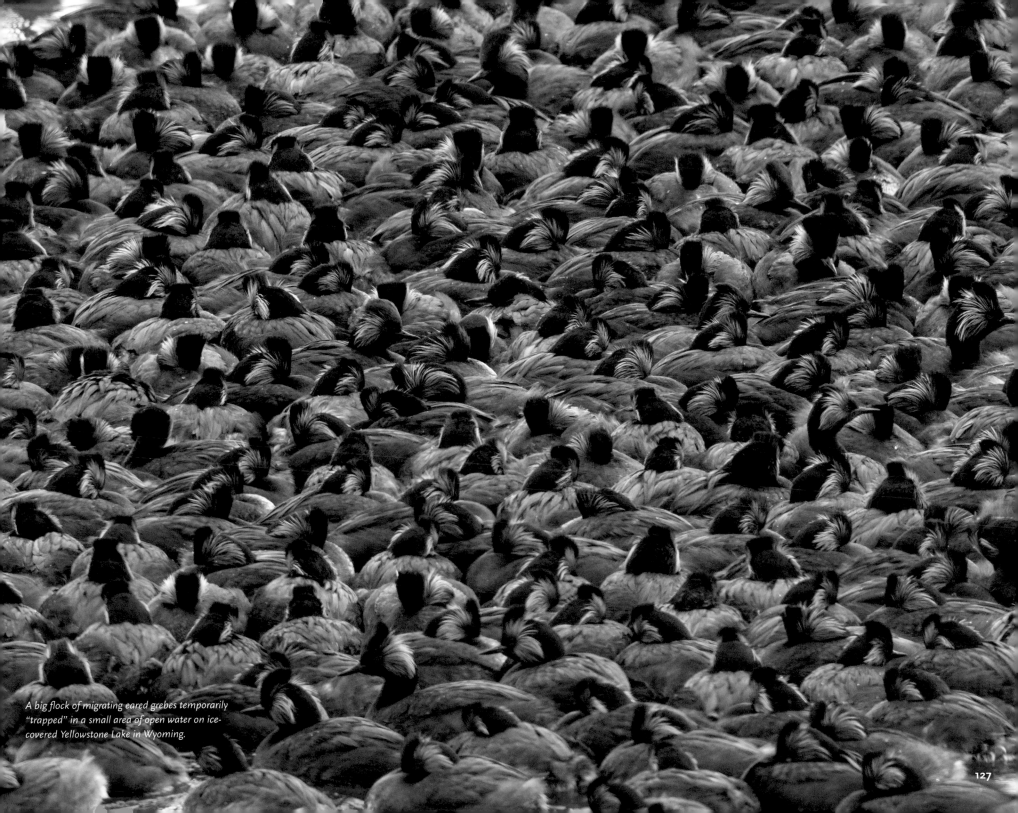

A big flock of migrating eared grebes temporarily "trapped" in a small area of open water on ice-covered Yellowstone Lake in Wyoming.

CHAPTER 9

Ocean Voyagers

An albatross is a great symphony of flesh,
perception, bone, and feathers, composed of long movements
and set to ever-changing rhythms of light, wind, water.

—Carl Safina, *Eye of the Albatross*

During springtime in the Alaska Arctic, common murres gather in a meltwater pool on the top of sea ice in the Chukchi Sea.

Seabirds are predators and opportunists, divers of the deep and roamers of the coastline, superbly adapted in form and function to thrive in one of the most challenging environments on the earth. Wherever major current systems converge along the Pacific coast of North and South America, seasonal upwelling delivers the nutrients necessary to support a marine food web of unparalleled diversity and abundance. The ability of marine birds to track the oases of life—the productivity hot spots—across vast expanses of ocean is key to their success.

Our fascination with seabirds takes us to some of our planet's most rugged coastlines and remote islands. On the windswept wilds of Alaska's Pribilof Islands, we encounter cacophonous colonies of cliff-nesting puffins, auklets, and murres. The flight paths of black-footed albatrosses lead us to nesting grounds on Hawaii's Midway Atoll, the tiny islands situated in one of the most isolated parts of the Pacific Ocean. For Pacific seabirds, the ocean is "home away from home." Land is simply a necessary inconvenience for breeding or roosting between foraging expeditions on the high seas.

The Pribilof Islands host the Northern Hemisphere's largest gathering of nesting seabirds, including puffins, auklets, murres, and cormorants.

Left: Laysan albatross chick in the nest at Guadalupe Island Biosphere Reserve, off the coast of Baja California, Mexico.

Right: Black-footed albatrosses haven't reestablished a breeding population on Mexico's Guadalupe Island or the Revillagigedo Biosphere Reserves in recent years but they are common visitors to both archipelagos. The core of their breeding population (more than 95 percent) can be found at Midway Atoll and other coral islands of the northwestern Hawaiian Islands

ROAMING THE OCEAN

Tracking seabirds with tiny geolocators and satellite-linked transmitters has revolutionized our understanding of their migratory journeys as never before. Some seabird species are short-distance migrants in the sense that their coastal breeding and overwintering areas do not require long, energetically costly flights, while many other species routinely cross hemispheres, traveling tens of thousands of miles each year.

The largest group of seabirds, the tubenoses—albatrosses, fulmars, shearwaters, and storm petrels—are legendary ocean wanderers distinguished by the hard, tube-shaped nostrils fused onto their bill. Tubenoses are unique among waterbirds in the importance of odor for nearly everything they do, and their nostrils play a key role in their ability to detect scent-rich patches of food as they roam the otherwise-featureless surface of the sea. Another distinctive tubenose feature is "stomach oil," an odorous liquid derived from the digestion of their prey.

Adults regurgitate the oil as part of what they feed their young, and both young and old eject it as a defensive response when disturbed. The pungent fluid infuses the birds and their burrows with a long-lasting musky odor.

Among the albatrosses, black-footed and Laysan are the species most often seen in the northeastern Pacific Ocean. It's thrilling when these magnificent birds appear alongside the deck of a ship, seemingly out of nowhere, gliding effortlessly through the giant wave troughs of the open ocean. Black-footed albatrosses are the largest and longest-winged of the region's oceangoing seabirds, and in the excitement of seeing one of these pelagic phantoms it's easy to forget that its 7-foot (2.1 m) wingspan is dwarfed by the 9-foot (2.7 m) wingspan of American white pelicans, inhabitants of inland and coastal waters.

Black-footed and Laysan albatrosses nest primarily in the Hawaiian Islands and in smaller numbers on islands off Japan and the west coast of Mexico. While raising a single chick, black-footed and Laysan albatrosses make periodic short and long journeys between their nests and oceanic feeding areas. During the early weeks of a chick's life, black-footed albatrosses make "short" trips as long as 200 to 300 miles (320 to 480 km) from the nest. After that, they begin making routine flights to the continental shelf of the west coast of North America between California and British Columbia, 2,800 miles (4,500 km) away. The full round-trip journeys are loops that cover as much as 9,000 miles (14,500 km) and require two to four weeks to complete. Laysan albatrosses make somewhat shorter foraging trips; they head north to the Aleutian Islands and Gulf of Alaska. The repeated long-distance foraging trips of nesting albatrosses far surpass the annual migrations of most other seabirds.

A female Laysan albatross, named Wisdom, was banded on Midway Atoll in 1956. She is believed to be at least sixty-eight years old, making her the world's oldest living wild bird. Although it is rare for albatrosses to breed every year, Wisdom and her longtime mate, Akeakamai, have successfully done so since at least 2006. The pair are currently raising Wisdom's thirty-seventh chick from an egg laid in November 2018 and hatched in February 2019.

The sooty shearwater uses its webbed toes to patter across the water surface in taking off.

Shearwaters are master voyagers, wave-runners that glide through the troughs, sometimes touching the sea with a wing tip. Although sooty shearwaters look a bit like smaller versions of albatrosses, their wingspan is actually much shorter than that of a California gull, even though each species weighs about 2 pounds (0.9 kg). California gulls are more buoyant in flight, but shearwaters can use their narrower, more compact wings to migrate across vast expanses of the ocean and to propel themselves beneath the water surface to catch small fish and krill. When we see sooty shearwaters offshore in western North America, and especially in Alaska waters, we can guess that they are at least 7,000 to 8,000 miles (11,265 to 2,875 km) from their breeding sites on oceanic islands in the Southern Hemisphere, anywhere from Chile to New Zealand and Australia.

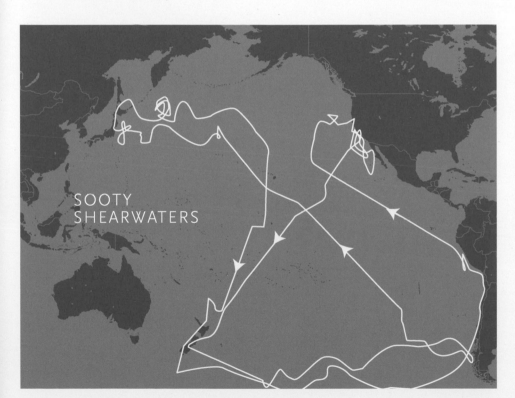

SOOTY SHEARWATERS

In moving between their widely separated nesting and feeding areas in the Pacific Ocean, sooty shearwaters follow circuitous routes that add up to nearly 40,000 miles (64,000 km) each year.

Floating plastic trash in the sea is an increasing cause of mortality for albatrosses and other seabirds. At Midway Atoll, the first landfall of the Japan Current, and on many other remote breeding islands, it is common to find plastics, trash, and discarded fishing gear in nests, along the beaches, and often in the bellies of dead adults and nestlings.

Pink-footed shearwaters—endemic to the Pacific Flyway—nest on only three islands off Chile. During the Southern Hemisphere winter, they are regular visitors to the food-rich upwelling waters off the west coast of North America, including the California Current. The global breeding population is thought to be less than 56,000 and is threatened by habitat degradation, predation by introduced species, human exploitation on the nesting islands, and commercial fisheries.

Fork-tailed storm petrels nest colonially in underground burrows and crevices on remote islands. Although largely solitary except during the breeding season, they may gather in small groups to rest at sea after foraging for plankton. Alaska is home to most of the population, with millions of fork-tails dispersing from breeding colonies in the Aleutian Islands and Gulf of Alaska south to California Current System waters.

Fork-tailed storm petrels are easy to identify with their silvery-gray plumage and dark eye mask. They are often referred to as the "swallows of the sea" for their close-quartering flight just above the water surface as they forage.

FLYING BENEATH THE WAVES

Some tubenoses can use their wings to propel themselves underwater in pursuit of food, but the true experts at underwater flight in the Northern Hemisphere are the alcids—murres, murrelets, guillemots, puffins, and auklets. These compact seabirds forage by diving from the water surface. With a forward tilt and quick flash of the partially spread wings, they push off with their webbed feet and down they go. Powerful wingbeats move them along fast enough to catch herring, sand lance, and other fishes—often one after another with apparent ease.

Alcids, such as this common murre, are sometimes called the "penguins of the north," but they are not closely related. Unlike the penguins, alcids can fly in air and water and, as you can see here, are experts at flying underwater.

When foraging to feed their young, rhinoceros auklets and other alcids hold one or more of their prey against the upper mandible with the tongue while nabbing another. A load of fish carried in the bill is typically delivered to the young at nightfall.

These male and female tufted puffins are performing the so-called "billing ceremony" with their bright orange beaks, one of several pair-bonding behaviors.

A crested auklet breeding colony is a feast for the senses—visually dramatic, loudly boisterous, and imbued with the scent of tangerines ripening in the sunshine. The citrus odor—strongest in the neck feathers of super-fit males—apparently plays a role in courtship behavior.

When compared to most other seabirds, alcids are migration minimalists, often frequenting offshore or coastal marine waters close to their nesting areas. The majority of the sixteen species found along the Pacific Flyway nest on cliffs, in crevices, or in burrows on islands or mainland coasts, returning to the sea during the nonbreeding season. Many tufted puffins and horned puffins winter in the North Pacific up to several hundred miles from shore in the pelagic realm of albatrosses and shearwaters. Juvenile puffins may remain at sea for several years before finally moving back within sight of land to join the nesting population.

Murres nesting on islands in northwestern Alaska (Chukchi Sea) winter in open waters near the Pribilof Islands and in polynyas near Saint Lawrence Island in the eastern Bering Sea. Polynyas—highly productive icebound ecosystems created and maintained by powerful tidal currents—provide seabirds with a critical source of plankton, krill, Pacific cod, sand lance, and other small fish. Polynyas have an uncertain future in a warming Arctic.

THE BILL FOR GOOD HEALTH

Vibrant orange bills and legs play a key role in the breeding behaviors of puffins and auklets, and both sexes develop orange "plates" on their bills prior to breeding. The bills of puffins are also enhanced with UV-activated streaks, which add pizzazz to pair-bonding displays. The orange color is derived mostly from carotenoid pigments, which the birds get from their diet of krill and fish. Research on puffins has shown that the more high-quality fish they eat during the nonbreeding season, the darker orange their beaks and legs will be. Carotenoid pigments are not simply conveyors of color; they are also a source of the antioxidants that regulate metabolism and stimulate the immune system. What is good for fish health is equally good for birds that eat fish. For puffins and auklets, luminescent orange is a blazing "health banner" that apparently signals breeding fitness to both sexes.

A few troublemakers can give any group a bad name, and so it is with gulls. For many residents of coastal towns, these birds are best known as miscreants, "seagulls" that frequent garbage dumps, fight over food scraps, and splatter objects and unlucky people with smelly "whitewash." But most of the millions of gulls and nearly twenty species in western North America favor natural habitats away from civilization. Some, such as kittiwakes and Sabine's gulls, inhabit remote wilderness and the open ocean and are familiar only to the most devoted bird enthusiasts.

Gulls are exceptionally adept at obtaining food, whether by plucking fish or crabs from the sea, harvesting the bounty exposed by the tides, snatching bird eggs or young, or scavenging carcasses. Some quickly learn to drop clams or crabs onto rocks, pavement, or rooftops, and thereby access succulent food morsels. Several species are aggressive on the wing and rob other seabirds of their meals. Shrieking groups of gulls often nab fish driven to the surface by feeding whales or take advantage of offal discarded from fishing boats.

Most gulls are short- to medium-distance migrants, but a few make long migrations. Sabine's gulls that nest on Arctic tundra wetlands in eastern Asia, Alaska, and western Canada migrate offshore along the eastern Pacific Ocean and winter at sea mainly in the rich waters of the Humboldt Current off the coast of Peru and Ecuador. One breeding pair tracked from the Canadian High Arctic took "separate vacations,"

spending their nonbreeding seasons in different oceans—the female off western South America, the male near western Africa.

In the Northern Hemisphere birds generally migrate south after breeding, but one of the gulls does the reverse. In spring and early summer, after nesting in the Gulf of California, Heermann's gulls move to the Pacific coast and begin a northward journey. By July or August, many thousands can be found on the outer coast and Salish Sea areas of northwestern Washington and southwestern British Columbia. The entire focus of northward migration is to feast on the region's rich populations of small schooling fish. In early fall these gulls retreat southward to northwestern Mexico.

About 90 to 95 percent of the total global population of Heermann's gulls (about a quarter million) nest on Isla Rasa in the Gulf of California, which is also an important nesting area for elegant terns.

This Franklin's gull is foraging from a dense cloud of brine flies along the shore of Mono Lake (California). Franklin's gulls nest in large colonies on prairie wetlands in central North America. During the boreal winter they crowd the Pacific coastal shores of South America, where flocks of 50,000 or more throng sites in Peru and Chile. Historically, flocks of up to a million birds migrated through central North America.

Terns are sheer elegance on the wing. The smaller species, whether hovering over the water or plunge-diving for tiny fish, seem ethereal and light as air. Larger terns, such as the Caspian and royal, are graceful and powerful fliers. Most terns make substantial migrations between nesting areas in the Arctic or interior North America and nonbreeding waters on the coast or open ocean to the south. Terns nest in colonies and may defend their eggs and young with intimidating attacks, swooping in fast and sometimes striking or defecating on intruders. Tern researchers quickly learn to wear hard hats and bring a change of clothing!

Aleutian terns breed in the northlands of coastal mainland Alaska and eastern Russia. With nesting completed, they opt for faraway warmer climes, migrating southwest 6,000 miles (9,600 km) or more over the open ocean to offshore wintering waters near Southeast Asia and Indonesia.

The population size of Caspian terns in North America has increased enormously over the past several decades, and the nesting range has expanded northward as far as Alaska. The growing population in the Pacific Northwest has put Caspian terns in conflict with efforts to restore populations of other migratory species—salmon. Decimated by detrimental effects of big dams, land development, and pollution, many salmon populations are now mere vestiges of what they once were.

The challenge is to find a way to restore salmon while maintaining resilient fish-eating bird populations. Caspian terns are fish eaters, and young salmon are a favorite, so managing terns and other fish-eating birds is viewed as a way of reducing salmon mortality and enhancing restoration efforts, particularly on the Columbia River. In years past hundreds of terns were killed each year as part of that effort, but now resource agencies actively manage Caspian tern populations by forcing the birds to relocate to nesting areas well away from the Columbia River salmon runs.

Freshwater marsh-nesting black terns follow inland and coastal routes during migration from interior North America to their winter range in marine and coastal waters as distant as northern South America. Large numbers spend the nonbreeding season feeding on fish in the productive waters of Panama Bay.

CHAPTER 10

Winged Messengers

For each of us . . . the challenge and opportunity is to cherish all life as the gift it is, envision it whole, seek to know it truly, and undertake—with our minds, hearts, and hands—to restore its abundance.

—Carl Safina, *Song for the Blue Ocean*

Migratory waterbirds link us to a world both ancient and wild—a natural heritage we share with all life on the earth. With their ocean- and continent-spanning travels, waterbirds are our sentinels in a changing world—each of their journeys revealing the fraying edges of the web of life that sustains us all. We face unparalleled environmental challenges in the twenty-first century, and the majority of these are the result of unrestrained population growth and human-induced climate change. The list of impacts is daunting—global warming, sea level rise, ocean acidification, overfishing and seabird bycatch, the spread of uncontrolled aquaculture, and the specter of chemical and plastic pollution in our oceans and on land.

Science illuminates our understanding of the lives of migratory birds, but science alone cannot repair the torn fabric of our shared world. The immediate threat to migratory birds is the ongoing loss, degradation, and fragmentation of the habitats they depend on along their entire migratory route. Although birds have the resilience to adjust to change, they need our long-term commitment to worldwide conservation efforts if they are to continue to find the habitats they need to survive, migrate, and reproduce across hemispheric scales.

Arctic tern

Long-tailed duck

Brant

Bridging the ever-widening gap that exists between our day-to-day lives and the natural world is absolutely essential if we are to inspire a love for nature and a conservation ethic that will stand the test of time and be our legacy to future generations. Many of the barriers to creating a "nature culture," as coauthor Rob describes the challenge we face, revolve around the modern cultural shift to an indoor-focused, technology-driven lifestyle. In conservation circles we often focus on "nature deficit" as it pertains to children. The disconnect between adults and the natural world is even more profound. Those of us who regard ourselves as "naturalists" often benefited, either in childhood or as adults, from a mentor, a teacher, or an experience in nature that helped shape our perception of the world around us. We all have the opportunity to be mentors in one way or another, sharing the delights and mysteries of the natural world—and migratory birds provide the perfect springboard for our efforts.

The dedication and hard work of biologists and conservationists the world over is rooted in science, but it comes from a wellspring of respect and love for their subjects. In the stories that follow, coauthors Geoff and Rob share their experiences of connectedness from their own "backyards," where they each conduct fieldwork. Audrey relates experiences on the Chilean island of Chiloé, where she learned firsthand what is possible when people wrap their arms around conservation problems that seem insurmountable.

Pigeon guillemots

Common mergansers

Late January 2017: a cold, cloudy day on the Salish Sea coast in Port Townsend, Washington. Using my telephoto lens to scan a line of brant resting and grazing along the shore, I spot a heavily worn color band on the leg of one bird. It looks familiar. On one side the code on the band is uniquely worn to the point of illegibility. Minutes later the bird turns, and I can see the inner side of the band—the white code on the blue marker is clear: TS5. I had seen this brant in exactly the same location in 2016 and 2015, and for the first time in 2012, each of the sightings in March or April. I surmised that this area must be a regular feeding stop or wintering area for TS5. Checking the banding records, I learned that this brant's migratory travels encompassed a far greater geographic range than my chance encounters would have predicted.

TS5 was banded as an adult in late July 1992 on Banks Island, Northwest Territories, in western Arctic Canada, at least 3,600 miles (5,800 km, as the brant flies) from Port Townsend. TS5 is one of more than thirty color-banded brant I've seen in this location, some in multiple years. Most of these were banded in Alaska and winter as far south as the Gulf of California, Mexico. The brant that appear annually in Port Townsend, in groups of up to 400, use the area to feed and rest before migrating north to their breeding grounds. Other sites in the Salish Sea attract many more brant, but the thrill of spotting "old friends" among these long-distance migrants so far from their Arctic nesting areas is hard to beat.

Epilogue: TS5, a male at least twenty-five years old, was found dead in the winter of 2017, just five days after I last saw him alive in the same location. Assuming that this senior citizen (brant sometimes live thirty years) wintered annually in the Salish Sea, its lifetime migrations likely totaled at least 183,000 miles (nearly 300,000 km), much more if it ever ventured to the wintering lagoons in Mexico!

ROB'S GLOBE-TROTTING SANDPIPER

To capture shorebirds for research purposes, mist nets are mounted on poles and stretched across a common foraging area to capture shorebirds for future research. The nets are made of a soft mesh, which doesn't harm the birds, and researchers are quick to remove them without causing injury.

The odds were 1 in 100,000—akin to winning a lottery. In the years before the advent of satellite tracking devices, spotting a banded shorebird required diligence and pure luck. Recapturing that same globe-trotting sandpiper along its migratory route was as rare as a snowstorm in the tropics. Spring migration fieldwork along the Fraser River Delta always brings surprises, but when I captured a western sandpiper fitted with a distinctive pair of leg bands foraging on a mudflat amid a huge flock of sandpipers, time stopped. One of the bands was color-coded to identify the place where the sandpiper was originally mist-netted (Panama), and the other bore a set of numbers pinpointing the capture location, a beach near the Panamanian town of Chitré.

My Panamanian colleague, Francisco Delgado, had banded many sandpipers along the Bay of Panama, one of the world's premier overwintering sites for Arctic-breeding shorebirds, as part of our joint study of western sandpiper migration. Disentangling sandpipers from nets is usually routine, but holding the banded sandpiper in my hand and staring into its eyes brought back memories of the tropical beaches at daybreak. We had shared the same air, sun, and beach, heard the squeals of terns, and watched scurrying fiddler crabs, and we had seen the men heading out to catch fish along the tide line. Our lives were intimately entwined.

Having extracted the western sandpiper from the mist net, the bird is then held gently in the hand and the open-sided, numbered band is slipped onto the lower leg and closed to keep it secure.

Roberts Bank on the Fraser River Estuary in southwestern British Columbia is a dynamic food-rich wetland complex used by vast numbers of migrating sandpipers, as well as other waterbirds and economically important fishes. Conservationists are concerned that expansion of port facilities may interfere with the ecological processes that make the bank so productive and valuable as wildlife habitat.

AUDREY'S CONSERVATION LESSON FROM CHILOÉ

It was November on Chile's Isla Grande de Chiloé, early spring in the Southern Hemisphere, and the ebbing tide had just exposed a seaweed-green mudflat at Pullao along the archipelago's eastern shoreline. Hundreds of Hudsonian godwits were foraging their way across the mudflat, poking their long bills into the muck in search of marine worms and other invertebrates. We were seeing only a fraction of the roughly 20,000 or so Hudsonian godwits (one-third of the world's population) that overwinter on Chiloé and take advantage of the rich smorgasbord of invertebrates these mudflats provide. The godwits were soon joined by large flocks of whimbrels and

sanderlings, and Chilean flamingos and black-necked swans fed in the shallows. These estuaries and wetlands are part of a 5,000-acre (2,023 ha) complex of crucial resting and feeding grounds designated as globally significant migratory habitat by the Western Hemisphere Shorebird Reserve Network.

Since I visited nearly a decade ago, the estuaries and bays along Chiloé's eastern shores had become a patchwork of salmon farms and polka-dotted with shellfish aquaculture buoys. Although initially welcomed as a boon to the Chiloéan economy, the fast-track modernization of what had once been a sustainable family-based fishing and farming

culture into an industrial-scale aquaculture phenomenon has had profound environmental and socioeconomic consequences for Chiloé. Despite corporate claims that industrial aquaculture is the way of the future and the Chilean government's efforts at imposing regulations, pollution associated with salmon farming is increasing at unsustainable levels. Toxic algal blooms are on the rise, possibly exacerbated by fish farm–related pollution. On the mudflats the soaring demand for agar, the jellylike substance obtained from red algae and used in the cosmetic and pharmaceutical industries, and other types of seaweed harvesting have exponentially overtaken the once-benign practice of collecting seaweed at low tide. Increased foot and wheeled traffic associated with seaweed harvesting is causing extensive damage to the mudflat ecosystems and the mud-dwelling invertebrates that many shorebirds depend on.

A very bright star has appeared on Chiloé's conservation horizon—a homegrown Chiloé-based nonprofit, the Center for the Study and Conservation of Natural Heritage (Centro de Estudio y Conservación del Patrimonio Natural), or CECPAN. Its mission is to develop research and education activities that promote the integration of citizens in the conservation of Chiloé's natural and cultural heritage. Promoting the idea that local people should have a say in shaping their homeland's future and environmental health has taken hold because of the community bridge-building efforts initiated by CECPAN's founders, a dedicated group of Chilean ornithologists and citizen activists. Their conservation efforts have gained the enthusiastic support of local communities, Chilean government officials, as well as funding and other types of assistance from a growing number of North American conservation and research organizations.

CECPAN is working tirelessly to develop school programs and community educational facilities on Chiloé, such as the Centro de Interpretación Ambiental de Caulín (Environmental Interpretation Center) at the rural school Luis Segovia Ross. The lovely ecosystem murals that decorate the center's outer walls and the student paintings of Chiloéan birds and marine life that hang proudly in the elementary school hallways are a part of this effort. Both buildings overlook one of Chiloé's most important estuaries. The center provides educational workshops and activities, as well as the annual Festival de Aves Migratorias, for children and adults that focus on local natural history, bird-watching, recycling, and traditional Chiloéan folklore, foods, and crafts.

149

EMBRACING THE CHALLENGE

Our goal with *Pacific Flyway* is to inspire wonder but also to portray the extraordinary lives of migratory waterbirds in their full range of habitats. Our lives and theirs are inextricably intertwined, and we—scientists, bird lovers, students of all ages, artists, photographers, writers, and all the rest of us—must embrace the conservation strategies and creative solutions that balance human needs with those of wild animals in their natural habitats. Although several conservation success stories in recent years give us cause for hope, we still have a long road ahead of us to ensure that future generations will be able to hear the "voices of migration." If migratory birds are unable to make safe passage through the landscapes we have claimed as our own, if they cannot find the food they need or the places of refuge they seek in an ever-changing world, we risk losing these fellow sojourners from our lives forever. The flight is leaving. Where will the birds take us next?

Elegant terns

ACKNOWLEDGMENTS

Pacific Flyway reflects the creative vision, scientific expertise, financial support, and encouragement of many people. We are thankful to Gary Luke, Sasquatch Books' former publisher and editor, for proposing a book that introduces a new generation of bird lovers and conservationists to the Pacific Flyway. The unique collaboration between Sasquatch and nonprofit Cloud Ridge Publishing (CRP) empowers an unparalleled level of professionalism and excellence in conservation publishing. Sasquatch's stellar team members—including Gary Luke, Jennifer Worick, Jill Saginario, Tony Ong, Alison Keefe, and Liza Brice-Dahmen—were unwavering in their enthusiastic support for this book and responded to our constant tweaking with consummate skill and patience. As always, we extend our profound gratitude to CRP's production team of Wendy Shattil, Ann Douden, and Alice Levine for their creative expertise and extraordinary work.

Our book is founded on the work of countless researchers and environmental nonprofits whose tireless efforts have illuminated the lives of migratory waterbirds and the challenges they face throughout the Pacific Americas. The dedicated scientists and conservationists who inspired us most as we worked on the book included: Brad Andres (USFWS); Fernando Angulo (CORBIDI, Peru); Patricia Baird, Robert Elner, and Ronald Ydenberg (Simon Fraser University, BC); Dee Boersma and Sue Moore (Center for Ecosystem Sentinels, University of Washington); Rob Clay, Salvadora Morales, Diego Luna Quevedo, and Brad Winn (Manomet/WHSRN); Mark Colwell (Humboldt State University); Claudio Delgado and Luis Espinosa (Conservación Marina, Chile); Mark Drever (Pacific Wildlife Research Centre, BC); Carmen Espoz (University Santo Tomás, Chile); Patricia González (Fundación Inalafquen, Argentina); César Guerrero and Jonathan Vargas (Terra Peninsular, Baja California); Juan Navedo (Universidad Austral de Chile); Gabrielle Nevitt (UC Davis); Eduardo Palacios (CICESE, Baja California Sur); Daniel Ruthrauff (USGS, Alaska); and Jorge Valenzuela and Gabriel Huenun (CECPAN, Chile).

Skilled local experts facilitated our field trips to see migratory waterbirds in Latin America. Raffaele Di Biase of BirdsChile showed us thousands of North American shorebird migrants and their crucial nonbreeding habitats in the vicinity of Isla de Chiloé, Chile. Carol and Carlos Passera (Causana Viajes, Argentina) expertly familiarized us with important migratory bird habitats in Argentina and Chile. Carlos Gajon personally shared his intimate experience with the waterbirds of Baja California, Mexico.

Cartographer Daniel Huffman and TerraGraphica's Eric Cline combined their expertise in providing the lovely base maps we've used in the book. We benefited from carefully archived data sources that allowed instructive insights into the lives and changing conservation status of migratory birds. Danny Bystrak of the US Geological Survey's Bird Banding Lab sent us original tagging data related to our sightings of color-banded brant. State and provincial natural heritage programs and conservation data centers of the NatureServe network provided information on the historical and current regional status of migratory waterbirds in the United States and Canada.

Mentors, family, and friends have played key roles in our lives as lifelong naturalists and authors of this book. Geoffrey A. Hammerson acknowledges his cousin, James M. Bates Jr. (1949–2014), for opening his eyes to the nuances among sandpipers. A. Starker Leopold (1913–1983) inspired him to become a biologist and taught him many things about migratory waterfowl. Howard L. Cogswell (1915–2006) expanded Geoff's knowledge of waterbirds around San Francisco Bay, and in his airplane gave him a sandhill crane's perspective of California's Central Valley. Robert W. Butler thanks Robert Elner for sharing recent information on biofilm, Sharon Butler for her support during the writing of this book, and Joe Gaydos for his encouragement. Audrey DeLella Benedict gratefully acknowledges Jim Chu, migratory bird specialist for the US Forest Service's International Program, for introducing her to researchers and conservation partners along the entire length of the Pacific Americas Flyway. Joe Gaydos, SeaDoc's chief scientist and Audrey's coauthor on two previous books, encouraged her goal of producing books that inspire the next generation of conservation stewards. Audrey's beloved friends and family, and Labrador Raven, brought sunshine to burn off writer's fog, nourishing meals, and continually buoyed her spirits. Our heartfelt thanks to all!

PHOTO CREDITS

CLOUD RIDGE PUBLISHING DONORS

Without the generous financial sponsorship and support of nonprofit organizations, foundations and individuals, this book would not have been possible. Our sponsors include the Benedict Family Foundation, Susan M. Bender Family Fund, Forterra, Center for Ecosystem Sentinels (Dr. Dee Boersma and Dr. Sue Moore), International League of Conservation Photographers (iLCP), Pacific Catalyst (Bill Bailey and Tracie Triolo), Whittier Foundation (Bryce Rhodes), Ann W. Douden and Richard E. Messer, Chris Moench and Jennifer Hahn, and Donald Van Wie.

Individual donor support included gifts from Dan Baker and Joan Ritchie, Bill and Mary Benedict, Bob and Margie Benedict, Bill and Margie Bernaski, Henry Bevington and Rosemary Andre, Joan Bevington, Sonya Binns, Diane Capron, Lynn Cooper and Bozena Nowicka, Leslie Dierauf and Jim Hurley, Dave and Mary Driscoll, Fran Enright, Scott and MaryJill Fransen, Ivor and Viann Hoglund, Mehry Khosravi, Rashid and Nina Khosravi, Judah and Alice Levine, Robert and Ginie Miner, Ellie Sciarra and Wolf Reitz, and Leslie Walker.

ABOUT THE AUTHORS

Audrey DeLella Benedict is a naturalist in the classic tradition. She is the founder of Cloud Ridge Naturalists, a forty-year-old nonprofit education and publishing program, and the author of several books, including *The Salish Sea: Jewel of the Pacific Northwest*. Audrey divides her time between the Colorado mountains and an off-grid cottage on an island in the Salish Sea.

Geoffrey A. Hammerson became fascinated with waterbird migration on the mudflats of San Francisco Bay in the 1960s. He has taught bird biology classes at the University of Colorado Boulder and Wesleyan University, and worked as a research zoologist for the Nature Conservancy and NatureServe for more than thirty years.

Robert W. Butler has studied, illustrated, and written about birds in the Americas as a Canadian federal government scientist, professor, and naturalist for more than fifty years. He is a fellow of the American Ornithological Society, the Explorers Club, and the Royal Canadian Geographical Society.